The Stock Investor's
POCKET CALCULATOR

The Stock Investor's
POCKET CALCULATOR

A Quick Guide to All the
Formulas and Ratios You Need
to Invest Like a Pro

MICHAEL C. THOMSETT

American Management Association

New York • Atlanta • Brussels • Chicago • Mexico City • San Francisco
Shanghai • Tokyo • Toronto • Washington, D.C.

Special discounts on bulk quantities of AMACOM books are available to corporations, professional associations, and other organizations. For details, contact Special Sales Department, AMACOM, a division of American Management Association, 1601 Broadway, New York, NY 10019.
Tel.: 212-903-8316. Fax: 212-903-8083.
Website: www.amacombooks.org

This publication is designed to provide accurate and authoritative information in regard to the subject matter covered. It is sold with the understanding that the publisher is not engaged in rendering legal, accounting, or other professional service. If legal advice or other expert assistance is required, the services of a competent professional person should be sought.

Library of Congress Cataloging-in-Publication Data

Thomsett, Michael C.
    The stock investor's pocket calculator : a quick guide to all the formulas and ratios you need to invest like a pro / Michael C. Thomsett.
        p.   cm.
    Includes index.
    ISBN-13: 978-0-8144-7460-0
    ISBN-10: 0-8144-7460-8
    1. Investments—Mathematics.   2. Investment analysis—Mathematics.   3. Business mathematics.   I. Title.

HG4515.3.T463   2007
332.63'2201513—dc22

                                                        2007010455

Printing number

10 9 8 7 6 5 4 3 2

CONTENTS

The Stock Investor's
POCKET CALCULATOR

THE BASIC DOLLARS AND CENTS PROBLEM

OVERCOMING THE NUMBERS

YOU HAVE SO MANY DIFFERENT WAYS of calculating "profit" or "yield" or "return" that no clear, simple answer will suffice. It is different in each situation.

Figuring out the mathematical aspects of investing money does not have to be difficult or confusing. It is made so by (a) the variation and unnecessary complexity of statements you receive from brokerage firms and mutual funds; (b) the cross-use of terms meaning approximately the same thing; and (c) the often misleading claims made in ads about the kinds of rates you can expect to earn (or would have earned if only you had invested five years ago).

None of these calculations are complicated at all. This book attempts to sort through the confusion and present you with a methodical, logical, and easy way to figure out the answers and interpret what you read and hear. Each chapter tackles a specific topic and provides examples of formulas in context. The topics covered include "returns" (return on investment and return on capital, which are not always the same); how leverage changes the equation; calculations over the long term; adjusting for what corpora-

1

tions report versus what is accurate; fundamental and technical analysis of stocks; and tax-related calculations.

More important than anything else, everyone should remember this: No investment calculation is so complex that you cannot figure it out. As long as you clarify what you are interested in finding out, you can crunch the numbers. At times, knowing the right questions to ask is the most difficult part of the calculation; so this book shows you how to go through that initial phase.

It also helps to think of these investment calculations in practical terms. Figuring out profitability is a method for keeping track of your investing success. So any series of calculations performed to figure out a percentage of profit has a specific context and purpose. Unfortunately, it becomes complicated if and when you compare two different investments without making sure they are expressed on the same basis. It is all too easy to arrive at a distorted answer. For example, if you own two stocks and make a net profit of 10% on both, that is an identical outcome—if you owned those stocks for exactly the same time period. But if you owned one stock for exactly one year and another for two years, the outcome is not the same. If it takes two years to earn 10%, that is an average of only 5% per year—or half as high as earning the same percentage in half the time.

Many adjustments, similar to this, need to be made in order to arrive at an *accurate* outcome. This is one of the major problems you see constantly in any type of financial study. Companies selling products make the issue more complex through the way they express numbers, often exaggerating outcomes to make what they offer seem more attractive than it is, or more profitable than it has been.

So when it comes to calculating outcomes, you are on your own. You need to take the information you are presented (or project into the future based on your own assumptions) and take steps to make sure you are using like-kind comparisons. So many investors make mistakes in their assumptions and basis for comparison, leading to a low quality of information. If nothing else, improving the quality and consistency of your calculations is going to help you to become a better informed and more confident investor. In figuring out likely outcomes, one purpose is to evaluate risks—not only of specific products but also in comparing one to another—and this is an essential step in making any decision. So the more reliable your calculations, the more likely you are to make *informed* decisions.

With the Internet, you can find a mind-numbing array of free information, much of it useful in performing investment calculations. Many Web sites will be included in this book to help you make calculations when necessary. But be aware that the Internet also offers a lot of misleading information and advice. One of the problems with free information is deciding which has value and which is useless. It certainly makes sense to evaluate information as broadly as possible in your initial research and before making decisions, but once you have narrowed down your sources and determined which kinds of calculations are valid and useful, you may discover that the large volume of free online advice is mostly useless in the decision-making process. A lot of it is promotional, and the useful information can be divided into a limited number of categories, including four primary areas:

1. *Information and background.* One of the most amazing things about the Internet is the availability of free articles and tutorials on a vast number of topics. Many of these are provided on sites trying to attract subscribers, and that is not a problem. You can read the articles and follow links without being obligated to sign up, and the Internet is an excellent place to get a free financial education.

2. *Definitions.* Another good use of the Internet is for gaining an understanding of terms. The investment arena has thousands of specialized words and phrases that have specific meaning and importance, and for the novice, this can be overwhelming. But the Internet makes it simple to look up words. For example, www.investopedia.com is a free site with many articles and tutorials and an excellent dictionary.

3. *Free quotes and research.* Numerous sites provide free market information. Most allow you to look up stock symbols by company name and then find the current stock price and chart. You can also link directly to companies and view annual and

quarterly reports online. This is very valuable. Before the Internet, investors depended on stockbrokers and mail to send away for annual reports, and often had to wait several weeks before receiving them.

4. *Calculators.* If you do an online search for some of the more complicated formulas, such as mortgage amortization, for example, you will find dozens of free calculators to simplify the process. For these more complicated formulas, you don't need to know how to figure them out (although you will be better informed if you understand the basic reasoning for the calculation). You can simply go to one of the free sites and punch in the raw numbers.

This book is designed for a spectrum of investors, from novices to seasoned professionals. Its purpose is to summarize in a single text the limited number of calculations everyone needs to be a better-informed investor. This involves three broad areas where calculations need to be made. First is the *basic investment calculation* involving your portfolio, the computation of yield and return you need to make in order to judge your success. Because you hold investments for varying amounts of time, it is essential to develop a method of uniformity, so that your calculations are truly comparable and consistent. Second is the range of *calculations used by corporations* in computing their profitability, cash flow, and use of capital. As an investor, you need to understand these calculations so that you will be able to track corporate reporting and outcome of operations. Third is a broad range of *stock analysis*, which is the means for picking one company over another. This occurs in two separate ways, involving fundamental analysis and technical analysis. The fundamentals are the financial reports and the study of them, and technical analysis involves a study of a stock's price trends.

This book is set up to break down the many calculations every investor needs into logical chapters and to then present information in context. Most people will agree that investment success is more likely to occur when your information is sound. Not only do you need solid information to know when or if to buy or sell; you also need to utilize intelligent formulas and tests in order to make informed judgments.

CHAPTER 1

Rates of Return on Investment

What Goes In, What Comes Out

E VEN THE MOST SEEMINGLY EASY CALCULATION can get quite involved. For example, what is your "return"? If you invest money in a stock or mutual fund, you need to be able to figure out and compare the outcome. But as the following explanation demonstrates, there are many different versions of "return," and you need to be sure that when comparing two different outcomes, you are making a like-kind study. Otherwise, you can be deceived into drawing an inaccurate conclusion. And *accuracy* is one of your goals in going to the trouble of drawing conclusions in the first place.

The "return" you earn on your investments can be calculated and expressed in many different ways. This is why comparisons are difficult. If you read the promotional literature from mutual funds and other investments, the return provided in the brochure could be one of many different outcomes.

This is why you need to be able to make distinctions between return on *investment* and return on *capital*. Your investment return is supposed to be calculated based on the amount of cash you put into a program, fund, or stock. Most investors use "return on investment" in some form to calculate and compare. The return on capital is usually different and is used by corporations to judge operations. To further complicate matters, *capital* is not the same as *capitalization,* so corporate return calculations can be difficult to compare. Return on capital normally means capital stock. Capitalization is the total funding of an organization, including stock and long-term debt.

Judging the Outcome—What Did You Expect?

All investment calculations are done in order to monitor and judge standards. You enter an investment with a basic assumption, an expectation about the return you will be able to earn.

In order to judge the quality or the investment and the reliability of your own decision-making capabilities, you will need to figure out how well the investment performed. In so doing, you need to be aware of some popular mistakes investors make, including the following primary points:

1. *The purchase price is the assumed "starting point."* It is an easy trap to believe that the point of entry to any investment is the price-based starting point. Thus, the assumption is that price must move upward from that point. No consideration is given to the realistic point of view that price at any given moment is part of a continuum of ever-evolving upward and downward price point movements. As a starting point, price does not always move upward. In other words, profitability is not the only possible outcome; the rate of return may also be negative.

2. *There is no possibility of a loss of value.* Investors also tend to overlook the possibility that they can lose money in an investment. But there is an unavoidable relationship between opportunity and risk. The greater the opportunity for profit, the higher the risk; this is inescapable. So picking the "best" investment is a matter of identifying how much risk you are willing and able to take.

3. *A bail-out and/or profit goal is not specifically set.* Too often, an investment is made with little or no idea about the individual's

expectations. Do you plan to double your money? Triple it? Or would you settle for a 15% return in one year? Equally important is the question of possible loss. How much of your investment capital will you lose before you cut your losses and close it out? If you don't set goals and identify the point at which you will close the investment, then you cannot know what to expect.

4. *The specific method of calculation is not understood.* It is difficult to determine whether an investment is a success or a failure unless you also know how the return calculation is made. This includes making clear distinctions between different types of returns, the effect of taxes, and how the formula works. All these variables have to be made consistent between comparisons or they will not be valid.

5. *The time factor is not considered.* You need to take into account the reality that not all investments produce a return in the same amount of time. The longer the time required (thus, the longer your capital is tied up), the less effective the return. So the time element is crucial to the comparison of one investment to another.

6. *The varying degrees of risk are not taken into account.* Risk is not only an aspect of opportunity; it is really the reverse effect of it as well. Opportunity for profit and risk of loss are like two sides of the same coin. This relationship between the two attributes is shown in Figure 1.1.

   Even so, some investors focus only on the "heads" side and invest with the profitability potential in mind but have made no plans for the contingency of loss. How much could you lose? How much can you afford? What criteria do you use to judge risk? For example, investors who base their decisions on fundamental analysis look for revenue and earnings trends and compute working capital and capitalization ratios. Investors who prefer to trust in technical signals check price volatility and look at charts. Whatever method you use, a decision should be judged based on potential for both profit and loss.

7. *Comparisons fail to include compound rates of return versus simple return.* In calculating return, there are numerous meth-

FIGURE 1.1. OPPORTUNITY AND RISK.

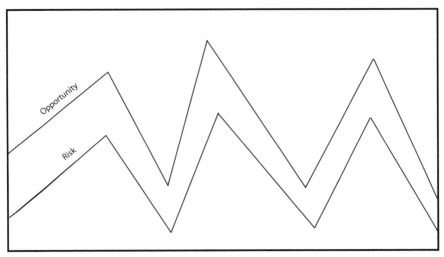

ods in use, and these are explained in this chapter. However, in estimating future returns, it is important to know whether you will earn a simple return or a compound rate of return. For example, if you are buying shares of a mutual fund, will you take your dividends and other distributions in cash? If so, your annual returns will be simple. But if you instruct the fund to reinvest your earnings, your investment account balance will increase each time you earn; the result is a compound rate of return, and over many years it will be much higher. So without deciding in advance how your mutual fund or stock earnings are going to be treated, it is not possible to set profit goals for yourself.

The important determination of an investment's success has two components. First is the decision as to how much profit you expect (or how much loss you will accept). Second is deciding how to compute the outcome.

Setting goals involves identifying the profit you hope to earn and, if you do not plan to hold your investments indefinitely, the point when you will sell. It also involves identifying when you will sell if the investment falls in value. At what point will you bail out and take a small loss to avoid a larger loss later on?

The second part—deciding how to compute profits and losses—is equally important because you need a consistent, reliable, and accurate method in order to assess your investing success and make valid comparisons between different investments.

The Basic Equation: Return on Cash Invested

Calculating return is perceived in many instances as rather simple. And it is, as long as the amount of money placed into the investment is the entire amount invested. In some cases, though, you deposit only a portion of the investment's total value, deferring payment of the remainder. Anyone who has ever purchased a home knows that the down payment is only a small portion of the property's total value; the remainder is financed and paid over many years.

The same thing happens with investments. For example, if you use a margin account, you are allowed to buy stock and pay for only one-half of the current market value. The balance is held in margin, and interest is charged. The concept here is that when a stock's price moves upward, margin investors make twice the profit (less interest) because they can afford to own twice as much stock. It's a great concept, unless your investments lose value or take too long to become profitable.

Another example involves the use of options, which is explained in greater detail later in this chapter. As one form of leverage, you can control shares of stock with the use of options for a fraction of their market value. So calculating return will be more complicated when options are used.

The most basic calculation is *return on purchase price*, which is simply the return you earn or expect to earn when you put the entire amount of capital into the investment. For example, if you buy 100 shares of stock and pay $2,587 in cash, you have paid the entire purchase price in cash. If you later sell for a net of $2,934, your profit is $347.

Return on purchase price is calculated by dividing the profit by the original basis:

FORMULA: RETURN ON PURCHASE PRICE

$$\frac{S - P}{P} = R$$

> where S = sales price
> P = purchase price
> R = return

The result is expressed as a percentage. In the example, the return is calculated as:

$$\frac{\$2,934 - \$2,587}{\$2,587} = 13.4\%$$

Return on purchase price is the calculation most investors are describing when discussing or thinking about their investments. It is the standard by which success is defined, and by which one investment is most likely to be compared to another. But what happens to the return calculation when you do not put the entire amount into the investment?

Return on purchase price may continue to be used as a common standard for the sake of ensuring consistency. But if you use a brokerage margin account to leverage your capital, you can expect two differences in the return. First, profitable returns are going to be much greater when you isolate the cash amount only; second, risk is also considerably higher. So the higher return is accompanied by far greater risks. Thus, it is not realistic to prefer using margin for all investing just because returns are greater. You also must accept greater risk levels.

For example, if your cost for 100 shares of stock is $2,587 but you deposit only one-half using your margin account, you may continue to calculate return on purchase. But you will also want to figure out your *return on invested capital*. In this case, only the actual amount invested is involved in the final outcome. The "gross" return on invested capital (before deducting margin costs) will involve a 50% investment, or $1,294. The formula for this calculation is:

FORMULA: RETURN ON INVESTED CAPITAL

$$\frac{S - I}{I} = R$$

where S = sales price
I = invested capital
R = return

Using the example and assuming a sales price of $2,934, your return would be:

$$\frac{\$2,934 - \$1,294}{\$1,294} = 126.7\%$$

This calculation is a theoretical outcome only. It is not realistic to count this triple-digit return as typical because not all investments are going to be profitable; it does not take into account the higher risk levels; and it ignores the fact that you continue to be obligated for the margin debt.

The advantage to using margin is that your capital can be leveraged. However, if a particular position loses money and you sell at a loss, you are still obligated for the amount borrowed. The return on invested capital formula is important in fixing the outcome, but only for a specific purpose: judging *overall* margin-based investing. So if you buy stocks only with cash, your outcome will be reviewed on the basis of the common formula, return on purchase price. If you use margin and invest only one-half, you double your opportunity *and* your exposure. A review of all outcomes on the basis of calculated return on invested capital will enable you to decide whether margin investing is more profitable or not. If your losses offset or surpass your gains, the added exposure to risk will not be worth the advantage (and greater risk) in leverage.

A third calculation that will help you to ensure like-kind comparisons in different markets and employing different strategies is *return on net investment*. This is the same calculation as either of the two previous formulas, but all outcomes are expressed on a net basis. So if you use margin, the actual profit is decreased (or loss is increased) by the interest cost of using margin. The formula is:

FORMULA: RETURN ON NET INVESTMENT

$$\frac{S - I - C}{I} = R$$

where S = *sales price*
I = *invested capital*
C = *costs*
R = *return*

For example, if your sales price was $2,934, the basis (amount invested in a margin account) was $1,294, and margin interest was $78, the outcome would be:

$$\frac{\$2,934 - \$1,294 - \$78}{\$1,294} = 120.7\%$$

An alternative method of computing this would assume that the margin cost should be added to the invested capital. The formula under this method is:

FORMULA: RETURN ON NET INVESTMENT WITH NET COST BASIS

$$\frac{S - I}{I + C} = R$$

where S = *sales price*
I = *invested capital*
C = *costs*
R = *return*

So rather than deducting interest costs from the sales price, they are simply added to the original basis. For example:

$$\frac{\$2,934 - \$1,294}{\$1,294 + \$78} = 119.5\%$$

This outcome is not significantly different from the previous calculation. However, the longer the holding period, the higher the costs—and the more important this distinction becomes.

Two final versions of return involve calculations with the dividends earned. First is *total return,* which includes a calculation net of costs, but adds in any dividends earned during the holding period. The formula:

FORMULA: TOTAL RETURN

$$\frac{S - I - C + D}{I} = R$$

> *where* S = *sales price*
> I = *invested capital*
> C = *costs*
> D = *dividends earned*
> R = *return*

For example, if your sales price was $2,934, the basis (amount invested in a margin account) was $1,294, margin interest was $78, and dividends earned were $124, the outcome would be:

$$\frac{\$2,934 - \$1,294 - \$78 + \$124}{\$1,294} = 130.3\%$$

The involvement of dividends is somewhat complicated, for two reasons. First, you are able to reinvest dividends for most listed companies and buy additional fractional shares rather than taking dividends in cash. This creates a compound return and makes comparisons more elusive. Second, the holding period will also affect the total return. If you own stock up to a few days before the ex-dividend date, you will not earn the dividend for the last period, which also affects overall return.

VALUABLE RESOURCE:

To find out more about reinvesting dividends in DRIP accounts (Dividend Reinvestment Plans), check the Web site www.wall-street.com/directlist.html.

The final calculation for return on cash invested is *dividend yield*, also called *current yield*. This is the rate you earn on dividends, calculated as a percentage of the stock's market value. However, a distinction has to be made. This yield is reported every day in the financial press and is based on the stock's closing price. But if you buy stock, your actual yield will always be based on the price you paid and not on what is reported later. So for anyone who already owns shares, the daily changes in yield are meaningless. The formula for dividend yield is:

FORMULA: DIVIDEND YIELD

$$\frac{D}{P} = Y$$

where D = dividend per share
P = current price per share
Y = dividend yield

For example, a particular stock closed yesterday at $48.86 per share. The dividend paid per share is $0.40 per quarter, or $1.60 per share per year. Yield is:

$$\frac{\$1.60}{\$48.86} = 3.3\%$$

The higher the stock's price moves, the lower the yield (as long as the dividend remains at the same amount per share), and the lower the price, the higher the yield. For example, if the market share price moved up to $55 per share, the $1.60 per share would represent a yield of 2.9% ($55 ÷ $1.60). And if share value fell to $40 per share, yield would increase to 4.0% ($40 ÷ $1.60). However, if you were to buy shares at the current price of $48.86 per share, your yield would remain at 3.3% for as long as you held those shares.

This calculation becomes more complicated when you reinvest dividends, creating a compound rate of return. Although the actual yield values may be quite small, an exact calculation would assume a continuing 3.3% yield on the original shares, plus an adjusted yield calculated at the time dividends were posted in additional fractional shares. For example, if you owned 100 shares and you received the next quarterly dividend of $0.40 per share, or $40; and at that time the share price was $42 per share, you would take the dividend in the form of shares, or an additional 0.95 share of stock. The yield on that 0.95 share would be 3.8% per year. (The $0.40 per share is a quarterly dividend, so it is multiplied by 4 to arrive at the annual $1.60. Divide this by the current share value of $42 per share to arrive at 3.8%.) The result:

100 shares earn 3.3% current yield

0.95 share earns 3.8% current yield

If this calculation were performed each quarter, you would arrive at a very accurate overall yield. However, with only 100 shares, the difference this makes would be minimal. For portfolios with many more shares, the calculation would be more significant because the dollar values would be higher as well.

Calculating Option Trading Returns

The calculations of stock return and dividend yield involve subtle variations. The key thing to remember is that comparisons should be made consistently between different stocks, funds, and other investments. The same level of calculation for options trading is far more complicated and involves many more variables.

An option is an intangible contract, a right. The owner of an option has the right to buy or to sell 100 shares of stock at a fixed price and for a very specific period of time. Once an option expires, it becomes worthless.

There are two types of options. A *call* grants its owner the right but not the obligation to buy 100 shares of a stock at a fixed price. A *put* is the opposite, granting the right to sell 100 shares of stock. Every option is tied to one stock, called the *underlying security*; and it cannot be transferred to other stocks. The *strike price* is the fixed price at which the owner of an option can *exercise*. When a call owner exercises that call, it means 100 shares of the stock can be bought at the strike price, even when the stock price is substantially higher. If and when a put owner exercises a put, he or she sells 100 shares of stock at the fixed strike price even though the stock's current market price is far lower.

In a nutshell, that is how options work. But because option values change as stock prices changes, not all options are exercised. In fact, about three out of every four options expire worthless. For the owner of an option, one of three things can happen: First, you can simply let it expire, in which case you lose the entire amount invested. Second, you can exercise the option and buy (with a call) or sell (with a put) 100 shares of stock. And third, you can sell the call or put and take a profit or loss on the transaction.

You can also act as seller rather than as buyer. In other words, instead of going through the sequence of buy-hold-sell, it is reversed to sell-hold-buy. Going short on options is far riskier than buying in most situations because you may lose more money than you can afford. One exception to this is the *covered call,* a strategy in which you sell one call while also owning 100 shares of the underlying security. If the call is exercised by its buyer, you have 100 shares to deliver; so even if the stock price moves far higher, you do not lose on the option transaction. (You do lose the increased market value of the shares, however.) You keep the money paid to you when you go short, called the option *premium*. The covered call is very conservative, and there are several possible outcomes. Analyzing these outcomes helps you to decide whether a particular position is worth the risks or should be avoided.

The calculation of profit or loss for buyers is simple. You buy an option, and later you sell it. The difference is either profit or loss. (If you allow the option to expire worthless, your loss is 100%.) Even though three-fourths of options expire worthless, they remain popular as side-bets in the market. This is true partly because the options market holds a certain allure for the more speculative investor or trader. However, options are also cheap. They can be bought for one-tenth or less of the price of stock. So rather than investing $4,000 in 100 shares of stock, you can spend $400 or less and own an option.

A comparative outcome is useful in identifying the attraction of options. For example, if you were to buy 100 shares of stock and the price rose four points, your profit upon sale (before calculating trading costs) would be $400, or 10%. However, if you bought a call option and spent $400 and the stock rose four points, you would double your money and sell for $800, or a 100% gain.

IN-THE-MONEY AND OUT-OF-THE-MONEY.

The illustration of an option's value matching the stock price point for point does not always occur. This is true only when the option is *in-the-money*. This means the stock price is higher than a call's strike price, or lower than a put's strike price. An in-the-money call will change in value point for point with the stock; as the price of the stock rises, so does the call's value. An in-the-money put does the opposite; as the stock's price falls, an in-the-money put rises one point for each point the stock loses.

The comparison between a stock's profit and an option's demonstrates the power of leverage. For $400, the call buyer controls 100 shares of stock, but without carrying the risk of investing $4,000 in shares. The maximum loss is limited to the price of the option. For example, if your $4,000 investment in stock falls to $3,800, your paper loss is $200 or 5%. However, you are not required to take that loss, and you can hold onto shares indefinitely. The option buyer, however, has to be concerned with expiration. The two-point loss represents 50% of the premium value. So while profit and loss can be far more substantial for options, their primary advantage is the lower dollar amount at risk. And the primary disadvantage is expiration.

The calculation of profit or loss for long positions is not complex. In comparison, when you go short with a covered call, your profit or loss is more complicated, for several reasons. First, there are three possible outcomes (expiration, exercise, or closing of the position). Second, because you also own shares of stock, exercise means that your stock will be sold; so you need to structure a covered call with the related capital gain on stock in mind.

The first calculation involving options involves selling covered calls and the sale of stock. Without options, the return on purchase price is easily calculated, because that price does not change. But when you sell covered calls, the outcome changes because the net basis in stock is reduced.

For example, if you own 100 shares of stock originally purchased at $40 per share, and you sell a covered call for 4 ($400), that may be viewed as a reduction in your basis. Most calculations of option return separate stock and options because it is complicated to try and figure out the overall return. But if you treat the covered call strictly as a form of reduced basis, then this calculation—*return if exercised*—can be very useful, especially in comparing one stock investment with another. The formula:

FORMULA: RETURN IF EXERCISED

$$\frac{S - I}{I - O} = R$$

> where S = *sales price of stock*
> I = *invested capital*
> O = *option premium received*
> R = *return*

For example, if your covered call was sold with a strike price of 45 (or $45 per share) and ultimately exercised, the outcome in this case would be:

$$\frac{\$4,500 - \$4,000}{\$4,000 - \$400} = 13.9\%$$

If the covered call had not been included, the two sides of the transactions would be calculated apart from one another. Thus, the capital gain on stock would be 10% ($400 ÷ $4,000). And the gain on the covered call would be 100% (because you received $100 upon sale, and it is all profit). But this is unrealistic; upon exercise, the premium you receive for selling a covered call reduces the basis.

The outcome may also involve keeping the call open until it expires. In this situation, the option premium is 100% profit; but it may also be used to reduce the basis in stock on an ongoing basis. You can write an unlimited number of calls against 100 shares of stock and allow each to expire in turn. Until one is actually exercised, you keep your stock. So the true net basis in stock could be viewed as being discounted over a period of covered call writes.

Finally, a covered call may be closed and a profit taken. When you close a short position, it involves a closing purchase transaction. Your original order was a sell, so closing this requires a buy. For example, if you sell an option for $400 and later close it for $150, you have a $250 gain, or 62.5%. You may want to close the covered call for a number of reasons. For example, once it is closed, you are free to write another one with a higher strike price and more time until expiration. That extended time means the option premium will be higher, so it is profitable for you to sell. Remember, upon sale, you receive the premium, so the higher it is, the more profitable.

The discounting effect of covered call writing complicates the calculation of return on your investment. But it also discounts your basis in stock and provides a third way to gain (after capital gains and dividends) from investing in stock. Computing your investment return is also complicated by the effect of federal and state income taxes.

▦ Taxes and Investment Return

There are two aspects to taxes that concern all investors: the *effective tax rate* and its impact on net returns, and the viability of tax-free investing (based on pretax and after-tax returns).

The effective tax rate is the rate that you pay on your taxable income. This is not the same as total income, gross income, or adjusted gross income. The formula for taxable income is:

FORMULA: TAXABLE INCOME

1) $I - A = G$
2) $G - E - D = T$

> where I = *total income, all sources*
> A = *adjustments*
> G = *adjusted gross income*
> E = *exemptions*
> D = *deductions (itemized or standard)*
> T = *taxable income*

This formula describes federal taxable income. The formula used by various states will vary considerably. The effective tax rate is the percentage that your total tax liability represents of your taxable income:

FORMULA: EFFECTIVE TAX RATE (FEDERAL)

$$\frac{L}{T} = R$$

> where L = *liability for taxes*
> T = *taxable income*
> R = *effective tax rate*

This formula applies to the federal tax rate. To find your overall tax rate (combining both federal and state and, where applicable, local income taxes), add together the computed tax liability and federal liability, and divide the total by the federal taxable income:

FORMULA: EFFECTIVE TAX RATE (TOTAL)

$$\frac{FL + SL + LL}{T} = R$$

where FL = *liability for taxes, federal*
     SL = *liability for taxes, state*
    LL = *liability for taxes, local*
      T = *taxable income (on federal return)*
     R = *effective tax rate, total*

The state-based taxable income may not be identical to the federal figure, but based on the rationale that federal taxes are normally greater than those paid to the state or locality, using the federally computed taxable income is the most logical.

To compute *after-tax income* on any investment, you need to reduce the gross return by your effective tax rate:

FORMULA: AFTER-TAX INCOME

$$I \times \left(\frac{100 - R}{100} \right) = A$$

where I = *income before taxes*
     R = *effective tax rate*
     A = *after-tax income*

By deducting your effective tax rate from 100, you arrive at the percentage of after-tax income you earn. This is divided by 100 to produce the decimal equivalent of the remaining portion of income. (For example, if your overall effective tax rate is 40%, you deduct 40 from 100 and arrive at 60. This is divided by 100 to find 0.60. This is the decimal equivalent of 60%, or your after-tax rate.)

There are many forms of investing free of income tax altogether, or with taxes deferred until the future. For example, municipal bonds are issued without a liability for federal or state taxes. But the interest rate is lower than you would earn from buying other bonds, so a comparison is necessary. By computing your effective tax rate, you can determine whether you would be better off one way or the other. The comparison would be to reduce the income on a taxable bond by your effective tax rate, resulting in your after-tax income. Is this higher or lower than the yield from a tax-free bond?

Another type of tax deferral is that earned in qualified accounts, such as individual retirement accounts. In these accounts, current income is not taxed until retirement or withdrawal, and, in some types of IRA accounts, you can withdraw your principal and leave earnings to accumulate without paying tax until later. In calculating a true and comparative return on investment, you have to consider the true net basis, the time the investment was held, and the tax consequences of profits. In the case of capital gains, a lower rate applies if the gain is long-term; this affects your effective tax rate as well.

Return on investment is far from simple or consistent, which is why you need to ensure that the methods you use are applied in the same manner in each instance. A much different method of calculations is used by corporations. When you invest in a company and examine the balance sheet, you discover that returns on capital are key indicators in picking the stock of one company over another. This is the topic of the next chapter.

RETURNS ON CAPITAL

PUTTING CASH TO WORK

THE INVESTOR IS PRIMARILY CONCERNED WITH calculating a rate of return on invested capital. "How much did I invest and how much did I take out? How long did it take? What is my return?" In comparison, the corporation looks at a range of "performance" returns in a much different manner. From a corporate perspective, use of capital and cash are more important than to the individual.

The two—individual investors and corporations—both want to maximize their available capital, and both are concerned with profitability. As an investor, you expect your capital to grow due to expanded market value. As a corporation, the expectation is based on profit and loss and how well that is accomplished. Corporate evaluation and judgment depends on many aspects to this question: competition, keeping expenses under control, identifying and moving into many different product and geographic markets, and keeping a sensible balance between net worth (equity) and debt capitalization (borrowed money, or debt capital). The task faced by the corporation in setting up and monitoring these aspects of corporate returns on capital involves a few calculations that are much different from those executed by investors.

▨ Calculating Returns from the Corporate View

The first question in the mind of a corporate analyst is, "How well did the company put its capital to work to produce profits?" This analysis is performed not only by the internal accounting or auditing departments, but also by outside analysts advising clients to buy or not to buy the stock of a particular company. So an analyst may make a recommendation to a client based on one company's superior return versus another.

This is not the same calculation as net return, which involves a study of revenues, costs, and expenses. In a later chapter involving fundamental analysis, you will be provided with a complete list of calculations to evaluate profitability on the corporate level. For now, the concern is with return on capital, the profitability expressed as a percentage of corporate equity. Corporations are responsible to their shareholders, who expect to gain a better return on capital from their investments than other investors earn from the company's competitors.

If the calculation were to involve only net profits and capital stock, the return on capital or, more accurately, *return on equity* is not difficult to calculate. The basic formula assumes (a) that the dollar value of capital did not change during the year and (b) that the calculation is concerned only with equity (capital stock). To compute return on this basis, the formula is:

FORMULA: RETURN ON EQUITY

$$\frac{P}{E} = R$$

where P = profit for a one-year period
E = shareholders' equity
R = return on equity

This formula is limited by what it excludes. It assumes that the value of capital stock is the same at the beginning of the year and at the end of the year. In reality, capital stock may change due to new issues of stock, retirement of stock (companies may buy their own stock on the open market and permanently retire it as "treasury stock," for example), or the effects of mergers and acquisitions.

The formula also is limited to an evaluation of equity. From a shareholder's point of view, this is valuable information; but return may further involve the use of debt. Total capitalization is the sum of capital stock and accumulated earnings, and bonds or long-term notes. So in addition to return on equity, it is also important to calculate *return on total capitalization*. This includes both equity and debt capitalization and presents a broader picture. Recognizing that corporations fund operations by selling stock and by borrowing money, this calculation can be revealing when tracked over many years. To calculate:

FORMULA: RETURN ON TOTAL CAPITALIZATION

$$\frac{P + I}{E + B} = R$$

> where P = *profit for a one-year period*
> I = *interest paid on long-term bonds*
> E = *shareholders' equity*
> B = *par value of long-term bonds*
> R = *return on equity*

Total capitalization includes both shareholders' equity and long-term bond obligations. So "return" consists of profit on equity plus interest on bonds. Although that interest is an expense to the corporation, it is income to bondholders.

Par value of long-term bonds is the face amount of the debt, which is also the amount that will be repaid at the conclusion of the bond term. This distinction has to be made here because bond current value may be at a discount (lower than par value) or at a premium (above par value).

This calculation is more complex than a simple return on invested capital (shareholders' equity) because of the inclusion of interest expense as a form of "return." But this calculation includes both sides of the capitalization equation, so both forms of return have to be allowed for as well. The balance between equity and debt capitalization is an important and permanent concern for corporate management. For the long term, a balance between equity and debt—or between production of profits and payments of interest— may decide whether investors select one company over another. The higher the interest expense (due to heavy debt capitalization), the lower the net profit. For the shareholder, this also means there will be less cash available in future years to fund growth in operations and to pay dividends.

Calculating Average Net Worth

The calculation of return on capital is easily performed if capital value remains identical throughout the year. The "return" is an annual event; in other words, the profits (or profits plus interest expense) occurring over a one-year period are simply divided by the capital stock (or capital stock plus par value of long-term bonds).

In practice, however, the capital stock dollar value does not always remain identical from the beginning to the end of the year. Because of this, the calculation is going to be inaccurate if it is restricted to either beginning balance or ending balance of capital. It is going to be necessary to calculate average capital stock value for the year. This cannot be done by merely adding beginning and ending balances together and dividing by two. You need to weight the average based on when the dollar value changes.

For example, if the beginning value is $4,500,000 and additional common stock is issued on March 1 for $1,200,000, the average net worth would be:

(2 months at $4,500,000 + 10 months at $5,700,000) ÷ 12
($9,000,000 + $57,000,000) ÷ 12
$5,500,000

The formula for this *weighted average capital* is:

FORMULA: WEIGHTED AVERAGE CAPITAL

$$\frac{(p^1 \times v) + (p^2 \times v)}{p^t} = W$$

where p¹ = period 1 (number of months)
p² = period 2 (number of months)
v = value
p^t = total periods (months in the year)
W = weighted average capital

If more than two periods are involved, they would all be added together and the total divided by the full year's periods, or 12 months. For example, assuming the above, if the company had also purchased its own stock on October 31 and retired it in the amount of $360,000, the calculation would have to allow for this reduction. Now the beginning year's capital stock, $4,500,000, would apply for 2 months; the value after the new issue of $5,700,000 would be applied to 8 months; and the reduced value of $5,340,000 would apply for the remaining 2 months:

$$\frac{(2 \times \$4,500,000) + (8 \times \$5,700,000) + (2 \times \$5,340,000)}{12} = \$5,440,000$$

The accurately calculated average net worth is used in the previous calculations of return on capital. However, the degree of accuracy you require depends on the amount of change during the year. For example, a significant level of change occurring in the middle of a month could make calculations of weighted average based on 12 months inaccurate. So in those instances, you can apply an assumption that all changes occurring in a particular month are assumed to occur at the mid-month level, and that the year consists of 24 equal periods. In this case, the previous calculation would involve adjusting the "period" calculation. In that example, the beginning balance lasted for 2 months and changes occurred in the third and tenth months. So the complete period based on 24 half-months would create a calculation assuming:

$$\frac{(4 \times \$4{,}500{,}000) + (15 \times \$5{,}700{,}000) + (5 \times \$5{,}340{,}000)}{24} = \$5{,}425{,}000$$

As a weighted average, this lower result would be more accurate if changes actually occurred on days other than the end of the month. Each month's holding period is doubled with the assumption that changes take place halfway through the month, so this accomplishes an average effect and avoids the assumption that change must conform to the standard of a 12-month year. The need for this added complexity should rely on the dollar value of actual changes as well as frequency of those changes.

The detail you employ in calculations of weighted average should depend on the significance and timing of changes. The *average* of anything should be computed to be as fair and accurate as possible. In the case of capital stock, new issues of stock or retirement of outstanding shares can be quite significant, so steps should be taken to make the average as accurate as possible; this explains the mid-month application in which the year is divided into 24 half-month periods. However, if you are going to compare formulas between two or more companies, you will also need to use the same weighted average formula in all instances.

Following is a simple Excel formulation for weighted average. The example is identical to the 24 half-month weighted average provided above:

Enter information in cells as:

A = period in the weighted average

B = number of months

C = value

Program formula:

cell	formula
B5	= SUM(B1:B3)
D1	= SUM(B1*C1)
D2	= SUM(B2*C2)
D3	= SUM(B3*C3)

```
D5      = SUM(D1:D3)
D6      = SUM(D5/B5)
```

Cells D2 and D3 can be automatically set by highlighting D1 and then pasting to D2 and D3. This is useful when many more periods are involved in the calculation.

The indicators above instruct:

:   add together the range of cells

*   multiply

/   divide

The outcome:

A	B	C	D
1	4	4,500,000	18,000,000
2	15	5,700,000	85,500,000
3	5	5,340,000	26,700,000
4			
5	24		130,200,000
6			5,425,000

Cell D6 is the weighted average. Using this formula, you need only enter the values in column C and the number of periods in column B, and the weighted average will result automatically. For example, you can easily revert to 12 monthly periods using this method. But because the formula is set, you could also use a much more detailed version, such as the number of days in a 365-day field. The use of the Excel formula enables you to simplify the entire process of computing weighted average.

Net Worth Versus Total Capitalization

Another range of calculations that affects judgment about corporate strength or weakness involves analysis of overall capitalization. How much of the total consists of debt? That is the important question that investors and analysts need to ask.

If debt levels are allowed to rise over time, the corporation will be committed not only to repayments of the debt in the future, but also to ever-growing annual interest. For shareholders, this threatens the future growth in dividends and also hampers a corporation's ability to continue funding growth and expansion. The more profits must be used to service ever-growing debt, the more restricted the corporation will be in the future.

The *debt ratio* is the calculation of long-term debt as a percentage of total capitalization. This is one of the key tests of a company and, although often overlooked, may be used to compare one company to another. To compute:

FORMULA: DEBT RATIO

$$\frac{D}{C} = R$$

> *where D = long-term debt*
> *C = total capitalization*
> *R = debt ratio*

For example, if total capitalization is $23.6 billion and long-term debt listed on the company's balance sheet is shown as $4.7 billion, the debt ratio is:

$$\frac{\$4.7}{\$23.6} = 19.9\%$$

For example, if you are considering investing in a retail corporation, you may check a series of ratios, including the debt ratio. As of September 2006, latest reported annual year-end debt ratios for four leading stores showed:

Wal-Mart (WMT)	35.6%
Federated (FD)	36.8
Target (TGT)	37.7
J.C. Penney (JCP)	39.4[1]

[1] Standard & Poor's Stock Reports.

While these debt ratios are within close range of one another, there are slight differences. This is one of several ratios that may be used to identify a "normal" level or even to eliminate one or more prospects from your list. For example, a check of four energy sector companies reveals a lower debt ratio percentage range, but a greater spread:

ExxonMobil (XOM)	4.4%
BP (BP)	9.6
Chevron (CVX)	13.4
ConocoPhillips (COP)	14.1

The ratio reveals that in the case of ExxonMobil, for example, only 4.4% of total capitalization consists of debt; the remainder, 95.6%, is made up of equity capitalization.

The debt ratio may be overlooked in the overall analysis of companies, and more information about this problem is provided in the chapters involving fundamental analysis. For example, some investors will focus only on the current ratio (a comparison between current assets and liabilities) as a test of cash flow. However, when corporations are reporting net losses, it is possible to bolster the current ratio by accumulating a growing level of debt. The borrowed funds are simply kept in cash, for example, to offset annual net losses. By doing this, the current ratio is not affected and investors whose analysis is limited to that test may be misled.

The solution is to check both current ratio *and* debt ratio. As long as both remain consistent from one year to the next, the conclusion that money is being managed well is confirmed. The purpose of performing any tests on reported corporate assets or liabilities (as well as profits) is to identify trends. But a single trend is not always reliable. When a corporation keeps its current ratio level by allowing its long-term debt to rise each year, it is creating future problems to satisfy short-term requirements. So confirming the apparent trend is essential. You confirm cash flow trends by checking both current ratio and debt ratio. By the same argument, the effectiveness of internal controls is checked by comparing increased revenues with expense levels, hoping to find improved margins. However, if you discover that the growth in expenses is keeping pace with higher revenues or outpacing that trend, it is a danger signal.

All financial tests can be confirmed by checking beyond the single ratio, and your ability to draw well-informed conclusions is vastly improved when you get a broader view of the corporation's financial status.

Unlisted Liabilities and Core Net Worth

One big problem in performing any tests of corporate health is that of reliability. Is the information you receive complete and accurate? In many instances, it is not.

An alarming reality about corporate financial reporting is the fact that some material items are excluded. For example, under the accounting rules (GAAP, or generally accepted accounting principles), companies are *not* required to list as liabilities their debt for pension plans. This is often significant. For example, as of 2006, General Motors (GM) owed more in current and future unfunded pension benefits than its net worth. If those liabilities were shown on the books, GM would have reported negative net worth.

The flaws in the system that allow such large liabilities to simply be left off the balance sheet should concern every investor. From an analytical point of view, this also means that it is most difficult to use published balance sheets for any reliable calculations of return on capital, debt ratio, and related tests of corporate strength or weakness. If small items are excluded or reported inaccurately, it does not have a big effect. But in the case of pension liabilities, GM's involved over $10 billion. Making matters even more severe, GM's debt ratio is 91%, meaning the company is funded 91% by debt and only 9% by equity.

Determining which adjustments, if any, are needed to make financial statements accurate is a tall order. Most investors are unable and unwilling to go through the 100-plus pages of highly technical footnotes to find all the adjustments that may have to be made; and even making that effort, there is no certainty that a nonaccountant investor would be able to decipher those footnotes.

In spite of legislation intended to make corporate reporting as transparent as possible, the current reporting format is highly unreliable and cannot be relied upon to produce dependable ratios or trends. To arrive at the "core net worth" of a corporation, it is necessary to adjust the reported value of both assets and liabilities. Because this may involve a great amount of detail, identifying the major adjustments may be enough. The formula for *core net worth* is:

FORMULA: CORE NET WORTH

$$N + (-)A + (-)L = C$$

where N = net worth as reported
A = adjustments to reported value of assets
L = adjustments to reported value of liabilities
C = core net worth

You may not be able to find the various adjustments required, and you may need to depend on the advice of a financial professional or a subscription service in order to identify what levels of adjustment should be made.

Failing the ability to adjust reported net worth, consolation may be taken in the fact that the inconsistencies and exclusions of GAAP apply to all corporations and to all years. With this in mind, trends need to be evaluated not only in their current year but as part of an ongoing trend over many years. For example, an evaluation of a 10-year record of GM's stock price, debt ratio, revenues, and earnings reveals a serious decline in results even though reported net worth is far from accurate.

A symptom of problems involving adjustments to core net worth is also found in the core earnings adjustments. It is a fair assumption that companies with large core earnings adjustments (from reported earnings to core business–based earnings) are also likely to have large core net worth adjustments. You will also discover that as a general rule, companies with relatively small core adjustments also tend to report less volatility in stock price trading ranges. The fundamental (financial) volatility reflected in core adjustments translates to a corresponding high or low volatility level in the stock price; and this itself is a key indicator. The evaluation of core earnings and volatility in the financial reports is discussed in greater detail in the chapters about fundamental analysis; for now, the point worth making is that calculating return on capital can be quite elusive.

This raises another question: Even if you accept the reported value of net worth as accurate, what number should you use for net profits? Most analysts simply accept the reported net earnings on the company's income statement as the right number to use, but a company-to-company comparison will be far more accurate and reliable if instead you use the reported core earnings for the year. (The easiest way to find this number is to refer to the S&P Stock Reports; Standard & Poor's invented the concept of core earnings, and it reports this value in the reports for each company it analyzes.)

The importance of using core earnings in place of reported earnings will also affect how return is to be calculated. The noncore earnings may be very real in terms of profit and loss but cannot be relied upon over the long term. By definition they will be nonrecurring and are often changes in valuation reflecting an alteration in accounting assumptions. So restricting your analysis to core earnings, the following revised formulas should be kept in mind:

FORMULA: CORE RETURN ON EQUITY

$$\frac{C}{E} = R$$

where C = core earnings (profit) for a one-year period
E = shareholders' equity
R = core return on equity

FORMULA: CORE RETURN ON TOTAL CAPITALIZATION

$$\frac{C + I}{E + B} = R$$

where C = *core earnings (profit) for a one-year period*

   I = *interest paid on long-term bonds*

   E = *shareholders' equity*

   B = *par value of long-term bonds*

   R = *core return on total capitalization*

▪ Preferred Stock as Hybrid Capitalization

The complexities of computing return on capital demonstrate the problem you face: Identifying a means for consistent and accurate judgment of a company's basic value is no easy matter.

Capitalization itself is an elusive concept for most nonaccountants. Even if you know the meaning of *capital*, distinctions between equity (stock) and debt (bonds and notes) capital are not always clear. But if you think of equity as a means of ownership with long-term risk/reward features (i.e., dividend income and increased market value), it makes the distinction clear. Bondholders do not stand to earn capital gains and rely on interest as well as repayment of principal.

Another risk factor is based on priority of repayment. In the worst-case scenario, a company going broke, who gets paid first? Because bonds are contracted and have priority over common stock, bondholders get repaid before stockholders. But one class of stock gets paid before even bondholders. Preferred stock is so-called because in the event of complete liquidation of the company, it is paid first. So the sequence in priority is usually (a) preferred stockholders, (b) bondholders, and (c) common stockholders.

Some types of preferred stock are described as "mandatorily redeemable," meaning the stockholder will be repaid at an identified future date, and there is no choice involved. Preferred stock is often referred to as a hybrid investment because it has features of both equity and debt. Mandatory redemption makes this type of stock debt. However, preferred stockholders are paid a dividend, which is usually fixed. Just as bondholders get a fixed rate of interest, preferred stockholders' dividends are usually identified in advance.

Preferred stock can represent a substantial portion of total capitalization, although it is usually only a small percentage of total capital. Tracking this factor in total capitalization helps identify ways that companies use hybrid investments. If the *preferred stock ratio* climbs over time, that could be a sign the company is trying to keep the debt ratio low while accumulating a form of stock (preferred) that is really more like debt than equity. The formula:

FORMULA: PREFERRED STOCK RATIO

$$\frac{P}{C} = R$$

> *where P = preferred stock*
> *C = total capitalization*
> *R = preferred stock ratio*

Remember, total capitalization consists of long-term debt plus preferred and common stock; all three are included.

The actual configuration of "stock" can be very complex, with multiple classes of stock involved, both preferred and common. In addition, "total capital" consists not only of stock, but of retained earnings, the accumulated profits and losses from prior years. This is also reduced by dividends declared and paid. So "total capital" for the purpose of the various return calculations should exclude current-year earnings but should include retained earnings less dividends.

Considering that dividends are paid quarterly, the need to find a fair weighted average can become quite important. For the sake of simplicity, an argument can be made that annual return should be made based strictly on the balance of the net worth section of the balance sheet as of the beginning of the year. This argument reduces the complexity of computations and gets around the question of ever-changing equity due to payment of quarterly dividends and issuance of new classes of stock.

When a company issues a new class of preferred stock, it makes sense to evaluate its characteristics. For example, if the class is mandatorily redeemable, it is actually a form of debt. To accurately calculate a debt ratio in the case where mandatorily redeemable preferred stock has been issued during the year, it is reasonable to change the calculation of the debt ratio to the *adjusted debt ratio* calculation:

FORMULA: ADJUSTED DEBT RATIO

$$\frac{D + S}{C} = R$$

> where *D* = *long-term debt*
> *S* = *mandatorily redeemable preferred stock*
> *C* = *total capitalization*
> *R* = *adjusted debt ratio*

Some justification may be made for including all preferred stock in this calculation. As long as you apply the same rules consistently from one year to the next and between different corporations, the adjusted ratio can be performed on either basis. If you do decide to move any or all preferred stock over to be counted as part of debt, this also alters your computation of return on equity. The formula for *net return on equity* is:

FORMULA: NET RETURN ON EQUITY

$$\frac{P}{E - S} = R$$

> where *P* = *profit for a one-year period*
> *E* = *shareholders' equity*
> *S* = *mandatorily redeemable preferred stock*
> *R* = *net return on equity*

Reducing "equity" to reflect nonhybrid forms only makes both the debt ratio and return on equity consistent and reasonable. When preferred stock represents a significant share of overall shareholders' equity, the return calculation is not reliable. If the corporation wants to use preferred stock in place of bonds (meaning a de facto form of debt), it will distort the traditional calculations, and these adjustments are important for tracking long-term trends.

▨ The Importance of "Use of Capital"

The return on capital calculations and tests of capitalization are best used as part of a trend. A single entry in that trend is not as meaningful as the long-term direction it is moving. For example, consider the ramifications for stockholders of GM's ever-rising debt ratio. As shown in Figure 2.1, in 10 years debt rose from 58% of total capitalization to 91% by the end of 2005.

The obvious problem here is growing dependence on debt, meaning a requirement to repay borrowed money *and* to pay ever-higher interest each year. This erodes profits and ruins future dividend payments for stockholders.

FIGURE 2.1. GENERAL MOTORS (GM).

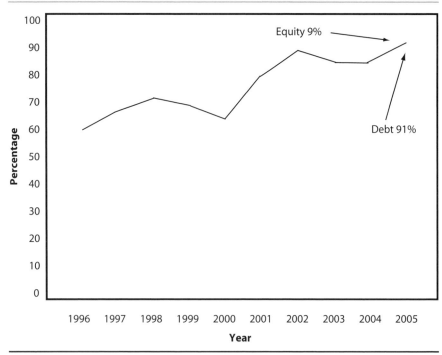

Source: Standard & Poor's Stock Reports.

This leads to another important financial issue: the use of capital. Whether that capital is derived from equity or debt, the corporation must be concerned with its annual cash flow. With 91% of capitalization represented by debt, it is clear that a great burden on the use of capital will be in the form of annual interest payments. If the organization is not profitable, where will it find additional money to retool plants, expand operations, or develop new products?

The best-known way to judge corporate management's effectiveness is through its use of capital. If management allows the debt ratio to rise over time, it is most difficult to imagine how management will be able to create strong and sustained growth in the future. Just as homeowners cannot expect to be able to afford ever-higher mortgage payments, management in a corporate environment cannot depend on endless profits to fund growing long-term debt.

The long-term trend in maintaining a cap on debt capitalization is one of the best signs that management is using capital wisely. Growth of current operations (excluding acquisitions or expansion into new markets) should be affordable from current profits. In the most ideal situation, a company is able to pay competitive dividends, fund growth and current operations, and keep long-term debt under control. For example, one of the best-managed companies on the New York Stock Exchange is Altria (MO), which sells the Philip Morris line of tobacco and Kraft Foods. Combined Altria is the largest tobacco company and the largest food producer. As of 2006, the company was paying dividends above 4%, which is exceptional. A look at its numbers shows that net income has risen each year while long-term debt has fallen:

	(In $ millions)		
Year	Net Income	Core Earnings	Long-term Debt	Debt Ratio
2005	$10,668	$10,766	$17,868	24.8%
2004	9,420	9,348	18,683	27.6
2003	9,204	9,348	21,163	33.0
2002	11,102	8,593	21,355	37.6
2001	8,566	7,959	18,651	35.3

Source: Standard & Poor's Stock Reports and Annual Reports at www.altria.com.

All these trends are positive, and the multiyear indicators support this. The only item that appears unusual is the gap between net profit and core earnings in 2002. But in that year, Altria sold its Miller Brewing subsidiary and received $3.4 billion, which explains the difference between the two figures.

It is clear that Altria has adequate current income to manage long-term debt and pay an exceptionally high dividend while its revenues and profits continue to rise. From the investor's point of view, the individual yield (from dividends) and the strong financial results make Altria attractive, especially compared to more troubled corporations, such as GM, with a 91% debt ratio.

This is not to say that borrowing money is a negative attribute. Most corporations borrow. But if the debt is allowed to run out of control, it foreshadows bigger problems ahead. Investors can learn valuable lessons from the corporate world in this regard, and can use leverage wisely to augment their investment returns. The next chapter explains this in more detail.

LEVERAGE AND RISK ANALYSIS

MAXIMIZING OTHER PEOPLE'S MONEY

THE CONCEPT OF "USING OTHER PEOPLE'S MONEY" is an appealing one. Many investors like to use margin accounts or even borrow money to build a portfolio. But an inescapable reality about leverage is that it comes with risk.

The correlation between potential profit and risk is a reality every investor needs to resolve. In determining your personal risk tolerance, a key issue is identification of the amount of risk you consider appropriate. That is determined by your income, assets, investing experience, family situation, and long-term goals. For example, if you are single and earning a high salary, own your home free and clear, and have a large cash reserve, you can afford to take relatively high risks in exchange for potential profits. But if you are married with children, are buying a home and paying on a large mortgage, and have limited income and investing experience, you need to move more slowly. Everyone has to equate their personal situation, knowledge, and goals with the appropriate risk level.

If you decide that leverage will work for you, then you will also be interested in some of the popular methods of leveraging your portfolio. These include simply borrowing money (for example, refinancing your home to get cash or applying for a home equity loan); using your brokerage margin account; and using options to control blocks of stock for relatively small cost. While there are many other potential ways to leverage your capital, these are the most obvious and among the most popular.

Calculating the Cost of Money

Are you willing to place your home at risk to increase your investing power? For many, the answer is no. When you refinance and increase your mortgage balance, you are increasing the debt on your home. When you apply for a home equity line of credit, it is like using a credit card. As you accumulate balances on that equity line, you add to your debt burden and to the amount owed for your home. The risk is that your use of funds may not be profitable. So if you lose money in the market, you have the worst of both worlds: You still have to repay the amount borrowed, but you have a depreciated asset in your portfolio. There is little doubt that anyone who increases the debt on their home intends to repay that debt with their profits, but there are no guarantees that the plan will work out that way.

This is not to say that leverage should not be used, only that you should be aware of the risks. It is important to determine that you can afford those risks before going into debt. The best way to quantify risk is through comparison of the cost of leverage, both between two or more alternative investments, and between leverage and nonleverage as separate strategies.

The calculated *interest expense* is the actual cost for leverage. The time element comes into this as well. The cost of a one-month move into and out of a position is clearly less than a full year's exposure. The time factor makes a significant difference; the longer you have to keep borrowed money outstanding, the higher the cost and the lower your profit. To calculate interest, the basic formula is:

FORMULA: INTEREST EXPENSE

$$P \times R = I$$

where **P** = **principal amount**
R = **annual rate**
I = **interest (per year)**

The interest rate is always expressed as a one-year expense. Thus, a 5% interest charge would express the amount of interest you have to pay over one full year. In the next chapter, you will see how different calculations of interest change the annual percentage rate (APR) you actually pay. If interest is computed annually, you pay the nominal or expressed amount. But if interest is calculated quarterly, monthly, or daily, the APR will be higher due to compounding.

In this chapter, the simple interest example is used. Simple interest is an annual charge only, so 5% means just that. Using simple interest, a 5% charge on $1,000 borrowed is going to be $50:

$1,000 × 0.05 = $50

Note that to multiply by a percentage, the interest rate is converted to decimal form. This involves adding two decimal places to the rate. So 5% becomes 0.05 and 35 percent would become 0.35. This makes multiplication easier to perform accurately, as long as the decimal places are included in the operation.

To calculate net profit on an investment, you need to deduct the interest expense from the actual proceeds. For example, if you invest on margin, you need to account for the cost of borrowed money in order to compare the outcome realistically. It would make outcomes highly unreliable to base profits on the full value of an investment when only a portion of the value had been placed; however, the interest expense must also be part of the equation. A formula for *return on investment net of margin* is:

FORMULA: RETURN ON INVESTMENT NET OF MARGIN

$$\frac{V - B - I}{C} = R$$

where V = *current market value*
  B = *basis (including leveraged portion)*
  I = *interest cost*
  C = *current market value at time of sale*
  R = *return on investment net of margin*

For example, assume that you purchased 100 shares of stock at $50 per share; invested $2,500 in cash; sold after a four-point rise; and financed the balance through your brokerage firm's margin account. By the time you sold these shares at $54 per share, your interest expense was $85. The net return would be:

$$\frac{\$5,400 - \$5,000 - \$85}{\$2,500} = 12.6\%$$

This rate of return points out the great advantages in using leverage. If you had invested the full $5,000, your $400 profit would represent only an 8% return ($400 ÷ $5,000). However, it is equally important to recognize the high risks associated with this strategy. For example, if you sold after the investment had fallen four points, the outcome would show a substantial loss:

$$\frac{\$4,600 - \$5,000 - \$85}{\$2,500} = -19.4\%$$

This loss is far different from a 12.6% return. However, it demonstrates a four-point move, but in the opposite direction. So in assessing leverage, be aware of the potential advantages and the risks.

Annualized Return

The associated potential for profit and risk is a feature of leverage, but another element has to be taken into account as well. How long do you keep a position open? The longer you have to wait before closing the position, the higher your interest cost. To make any comparisons truly valid, you need to consider the time element. A 5% cost over 12 months is just that, 5%. But if it takes only three months (one-fourth of the full year) to complete and close a position, your actual cost will be only 1.25%. It is still an *annual* rate of 5%, but only over one-fourth of a full year. On the other hand, if it takes 15 months to finalize a leveraged transaction, your cost will cover $1^1/_4$ years. So that 5% per year comes out to be 6.25% overall (again, still 5% *per year* but a higher overall cost).

To make any investments comparable to one another, the net return has to be expressed on an annualized basis. How much would your net profit be if held for exactly one year? How much would the interest expense be? Annualizing can be applied both to cost and to net profit (or loss). To compute *annualized rate*, divide the rate by the number of months the position was open, and then multiply by 12 (months):

FORMULA: ANNUALIZED RATE

$$\frac{R}{M} \times 12 = A$$

> *where R = net return*
> *M = months the position was open*
> *A = annualized yield*

For example, if you opened two different positions and sold both once you had made a 10% profit, are these identical outcomes? If you owned one stock for 7 months and the other for 14 months, the annualized returns are quite different.

To annualize 10% over 7 months:

$$\frac{10\%}{7} \times 12 = 17.1\%$$

Over 14 months:

$$\frac{10\%}{14} \times 12 = 8.6\%$$

This example demonstrates that the longer the holding period, the lower the annualized return. Using months as a base for calculation is the easiest method. You can estimate partial months by assuming a four-week period per month. So if you own a stock for three months and a week, that would be 3.25 months; if 6 months and 3 weeks, it would be 6.75 months. As long as you are consistent in these calculations, stock-to-stock comparisons will be accurate. You can also perform annualization using the number of weeks and multiplying by 52; or even the exact number of days a position is owned, with a multiplier of 365.

You also will need to keep comparisons realistic. Everyone knows that extremely short-term holding periods are not reliably profitable, so it is not accurate to use a strict form of annualization to draw conclusions. For example, let's say you invest $5,000 in a stock and sell one week later for $5,400. If you annualize on either a monthly or a weekly basis, the annualized return is impressive. The $400 represents an 8% return ($400 ÷ $5,000), but when you annualize, it is much higher:

Monthly basis (one-quarter month)

$$\frac{8\%}{0.25} \times 12 = 384\%$$

Weekly basis (52 weeks)

$$\frac{8\%}{1} \times 52 = 416\%$$

No one would expect to consistently duplicate this outcome. It would be unlikely that you would be able to produce similar profits every week for the next year. It is just as likely that you could have as many one-week 8% losses as profits. The point to be remembered here is that annualization is a useful tool for expressing comparative returns realistically; it is of no value when the holding period is extremely short or when the return is exceptionally high.

Leverage-Based Risk—the P/E Ratio as a Way to Quantify

It is all too easy to look at the rare double-digit or triple-digit annualized return, and to become convinced that these levels of profit are typical. They are not. The difficulty in contending with higher than average returns is factoring in the risk. That would make it easier to compare different returns and risks realistically.

Stocks that move rapidly either upward or downward—the more volatile issues—are by definition higher risks. Profits may be short-term and higher than average, but so might losses. Valuation risk—the risk that a particular stock could be overvalued at the time you buy—is probably the most common of all risks. The advice to "buy low and sell high" is profound because so many people do exactly the opposite. When stock prices rise, more people want to get in on the action, so the tendency to buy at the very height of the price curve can be strong. Likewise, when prices fall, investors might panic and sell at the depth of the same price curve. So a common pattern is to "buy high and sell low" instead.

To judge valuation risk, one formula that can be extremely helpful is the *price/earnings ratio,* or the P/E. This is a comparison between the price (a technical indicator that is very current) and earnings per share (a fundamental indicator that may be dated). To compute:

FORMULA: PRICE/EARNINGS RATIO

$$\frac{P}{E} = R$$

> *where P = price per share*
> *E = earnings per share*
> *R = P/E ratio*

This ratio is so significant because it can be used to judge whether a stock's price is "too high" if we assume some standards. The P/E is also called a *multiple* of earnings. The result of this formula tells you how many multiples of earnings are represented in the current price. For example, if today's price is $32 per share and the most recently reported earnings per share (EPS) was $2.90, the P/E is:

$$\frac{32}{2.90} = 11$$

Today's price is equal to 11 times earnings. This tells you a lot, given the following qualifications of the P/E ratio:

1. *EPS is historical and may be out of date.* If you are reviewing P/E three months after the end of a company's fiscal year, you are using outdated earnings information, especially in cyclical industries. For example, in the retail sector, the fourth quarter is usually the most profitable. So if your latest published EPS is for December 31, but the current price is as of March 15, the two sides of the equation are not as closely related as you might prefer.

2. *EPS counts only one form of capitalization.* The EPS includes only earnings per common share of stock. So in situations where debt capitalization is quite high, earnings are reduced by higher than average interest expense. When a company has issued a large volume of preferred stock, it also distorts the true EPS value.

3. *Current market value could be untypical.* If today's stock price is a spike above or below the more typical trading range, it is not reliable for calculating P/E. It makes more sense to base P/E calculations on an established mid-range price of the stock. For example, if the stock has been trading between $25 and $35 per share but today's price spiked to $39, using the $39 value for P/E is unrealistic (especially since earnings are historical). It would be more accurate to use a mid-range price of $30 per share.

4. *Tracking indicators by moment in time is unreliable.* No single indicator can be used reliably without also tracking how it has evolved over time. For cyclical stocks, a review of quarter-end P/E is more revealing than today's single P/E outcome. In this way, you can see how P/E has changed over time, and you can also recognize cyclical changes. By using historical data, you are also able to match quarter-ending price with quarter-ending earnings, which overcomes the big problem with

moment-in-time analysis, where the two factors are mismatched.

Given the problems of the P/E ratio, if you ensure that your use of P/E and earnings is accurate and well matched, you can make valid comparisons. The higher the P/E is found to be, the greater the chance of an inflated stock price. Returning to our previous example, the formula shown was:

$$\frac{32}{2.90} = 11$$

If the stock price were to rise over time, the P/E would rise as well, but the established latest EPS remains the same:

$42 \div 2.90 = 14.5$
$52 \div 2.90 = 17.9$
$62 \div 2.90 = 21.4$

Note that in the latest example, the price of $62 per share is over 21 times current earnings. Over long periods of time, lower-P/E stocks have tended to outperform higher-P/E stocks. The market tends to overvalue stocks when those stocks are in favor; thus prices may be driven too high. From the individual investor's point of view, this valuation risk can be quantified by comparing P/E levels among several stocks, as one of several means for selection. For example, you can make a rule for yourself that you will not buy any stock whose P/E is greater than 15. This level is provided as an example only. However, you will discover that a comparative analysis of P/E shows that stocks with exceptionally low P/E may be conservative choices, but the chances for profit will be limited as well, and that exceptionally high P/E stocks tend to be more volatile than average.

A reasonable conclusion is that picking mid-range P/E stocks is a sensible way to reduce valuation risk. It is not foolproof, but it is the closest thing to a formula that allows you to quantify the relationship between risk and reward.

One way to make good use of the P/E is to limit your range of comparisons between stocks. If you were to study all stocks in a single sector, you would be likely to find variation among the P/E levels. If you ignore these variations, you gain no insight into how or why to pick one stock over another. However, if you further limit your comparison to those stocks with P/E between 11 and 16, your list narrows considerably. It eliminates stocks of little immediate interest in the market as well as those with greater price volatility. By limiting the range of P/E, you also are better able to analyze valuation risk between stocks in different sectors. For example, you have the means with P/E to compare valuation risk between retail, energy, and pharmaceutical issues. While the attributes of these sectors are vastly dissimilar, valuation risk through P/E is far more uniform. Given the need to ensure accuracy and reliability of both the EPS and current price levels employed, this comparative study is useful.

When the study is used in conjunction with an analysis of debt ratio, revenue and earnings, and other fundamental tests, valid comparisons between stocks are more reliable and realistic. The P/E, like all ratios, is useful when viewed over a period of time and when the factors employed are matched in time.

When comparing stocks using P/E as one of the analytical tools for the task, be aware of other types of risk worth considering. These include business risk (critical analysis of a company's solvency, gained from bond ratings, profitability, and capitalization trends) and basic market risk (the timing of your investment decision). Many tools, both fundamental and technical, can help in reducing these risks. For example, technical investors use specific chart patterns to time their decisions. While this is extremely short-term in a strategic sense, timing a buy or sell decision can help you to avoid poor timing. Swing traders, for example, use a limited number of charting patterns to recognize and anticipate when prices are about to turn.

VALUABLE RESOURCE:

Swing traders use candlestick charts to identify buy or sell signals. For free educational information about candlesticks and free charts, check www.candlestickchart.com.

Swing trading is only one of many technical methods traders employ. A subset of day trading, swing traders generally prefer to identify trends evolving over a two- to five-day period. Fundamental investors rely more on financial information and view short-term price as chaotic and unpredictable. Both technical and fundamental sides can offer valuable and useful information to improve trading profits, which is why an indicator like the P/E (which uses both fundamental and technical information) is so popular.

Using Options as a Form of Leverage

One purpose in evaluating the mathematical returns on specific strategies is to help identify the risk involved. The P/E is useful in some respects because it can be used to compare stocks to one another, and to modify perceptions of profit potential. The greater the profit potential appears to be, the greater the risk. When you compare P/Es between stocks, you can also observe a correlation between interest in the market (higher than average volume and more volatile trading range, for example) and higher than average P/E. This is a good example of matching between profit and risk of a decision.

The options market allows you to manage risks while continuing to seek profits, *and* to use leverage while managing the amount of capital placed at risk. This often overlooked feature makes options one of the best vehicles for a leveraged strategy.

Since an option is a wasting asset (meaning it will expire in the future), it cannot be compared to the purchase of stock in every respect. As a stockholder, you can afford to keep a long position open as long as you wish, and wait for the price to rise. You also earn dividends as long as you own the stock. With options, there are no dividends, and expiration is an ever-present problem.

On the other side of the analysis, you can control 100 shares of stock for a small fraction of the cost of buying stock in the traditional manner. The price of the option varies based on proximity between strike price and current price; time to go until expiration; and the volatility in trading on the stock. These three elements are intrinsic value, time value, and extrinsic value:

1. *Intrinsic value* is any portion of the option premium "in the money." Call options are in the money whenever the current value of stock is higher than the strike price of the call. For example, if the strike price is 55 and the current market value is $57 per share, there are two points of intrinsic value in that call. For puts, it is the opposite. For example, if the strike price of a put is 55 and the stock is currently at $52, the put has three points of in-the-money value.

2. *Time value* is the actual value of time itself. The longer the time to go until the expiration date arrives, the higher the time value. As expiration approaches, time value evaporates, so that on expiration day, it falls to zero.

3. *Extrinsic value* is most often simply lumped in with time value and explained as a variable based on stock volatility. However, there is an element related to interest in the stock, and just as stocks are more volatile with broader trading ranges, options are going to follow that same tendency. So when you look at identical options on two different stocks—expiring at the same time, with the same strike price, and with similar or identical proximity to current value—why is the option value different? The answer is found in extrinsic value, that portion of premium reflecting the risk factor.

With option valuation as elusive as it is, one way to approach the leverage potential of options is to consider profit potential with various strategies, but in a comparative manner. This is the only reliable way to develop sound judgment about the potential and risk of one option over another or between options in general versus stock purchase.

The calculation of a simple purchase and sale of an option is not complicated. It works the same as return on investment for stock purchase. There are two elements: the first is the percentage of return, and the second is the annualization of that return. In the typical transaction, a trader buys a call or a put and closes the position before expiration. The net difference between purchase and sale price is profit or loss. Calculation for *return on long options* is:

FORMULA: RETURN ON LONG OPTIONS

$$\frac{S - P}{P} = R$$

where S = closing net sales price
P = opening net purchase price
R = net return

For example, if you buy a call at 6 ($600) and three months later close the position at a net of 8 ($800), the net return is $200, or:

$$\frac{\$800 - \$600}{\$600} = 33.3\%$$

To annualize this return, divide by the number of months held, and multiply by 12:

$$\frac{33.3\%}{3} \times 12 = 133.2\%$$

Remember, however, that when you annualize and end up with a triple-digit return, the calculation is of limited value. It is useful for comparisons, but it is not indicative of an outcome you should expect to duplicate consistently.

However, this annualized return does demonstrate the optimal positive outcome of a long position. Historically, 75% of all options expire worthless, so this exceptionally high return has a trade-off. The great advantage to buying options is that for the period those options are held, the buyer has the right to buy or sell 100 shares of the underlying stock at the fixed strike price, no matter what the market price of the stock. Additionally, risk is strictly limited. You can lose only the amount of the option premium and no more. In this example, the maximum risk was $600. Were you to buy stock instead, the entire amount invested is at risk. There is no expiration involved, but capital has to be committed, and, even employing leverage through a margin account, there is an ongoing interest expense to consider in the overall comparison.

Calculations for short positions in options are far more complex. The potential profits are higher than for long options, but the risks are also entirely different. Based on the specific strategy you employ, short options can be high risk or extremely conservative. A summary of this range of risks:

1. *Uncovered calls* are the highest-risk strategy possible using options. In theory, a stock's price could rise indefinitely, so when you have sold a call, you could face an undefined risk. If the call is exercised, you are on the hook for the difference between the strike price and the current market value (minus the premium you were paid). For example, you sell an uncovered call and receive a premium of 6 ($600). The strike price is 40. However, the stock soars to $62 per share and the call is exercised. Your loss is:

Current market value	$6,200
Less: strike price	4,000
Loss on stock	$2,200
Less: Premium for short call	− 600
Net loss	$1,600

The loss level depends on the movement in the stock. And because 75% of all options expire worthless, there may be only a small chance of exercise. Even so, an uncovered short call is a high-risk strategy.

2. *Covered calls.* When you own 100 shares of stock and sell a call, it is "covered" because you can sell the stock to satisfy exercise. Because of this, the covered call is a very conservative strategy. Your only potential loss is increased value in the stock if and when the stock rises. Upon exercise, the stock must be given up at the strike price. For example, if you sell a covered call with a strike price of 50 and the stock rises to 62, upon exercise, you get only $50 per share. However, the maximum loss is reduced by the amount you receive for selling the call. For example, if you were paid $400 in call premium, your loss before transaction charges is only $800:

Current market value of stock	$6,200
Less: Strike price value	− 5,000
Loss on stock	$1,200
Less: call premium	− 400
Net loss	$ 800

Selling a covered call produces immediate income, but the transaction is not taxed until one of three events occurs: your closing the position with a closing purchase transaction, exercise of the call, or expiration. So it is entirely possible to receive proceeds in one year and not be taxed until the following year.

The covered call can also be looked at as a discount in your basis, and thus, a reduction of market risk. If you purchase 100 shares at $50 per share and sell a call for 4 ($400), your basis in the stock is reduced to $4,600. So describing covered calls as conservative is intended as a comparative analysis. On the one hand, owning shares exposes you to market risk as well as offering the potential for gain. But owning shares and selling a covered call reduces your basis in the stock and provides an income stream; the major risk is lost opportunity if and when the stock's price rises.

3. *Ratio write.* A variation on call writing involves partial coverage. The ratio write involves covering a portion of your total holdings while including a portion of uncovered options as well. For example, if you own 300 shares of stock and sell four calls, you create a ratio write. You can think of this as 75% cover or as two separate components with three covered calls and one uncovered call. The ratio write can be built to eliminate the uncovered risk by purchasing one call above the strike price of the short calls. This works if and when the income from the short calls exceeds the cost of the one long call. Thus, if all four calls were exercised, the entire ratio write is covered by (a) 300 shares of stock and (b) one long call.

4. *Uncovered put.* A put cannot be covered in the same manner as a call. In theory, an investor who has gone short on 100 shares of stock could "cover" the position with a short put, but the

outcome would not be favorable. Costs would offset any miti-gating features. Additionally, with so many potential option po-sitions available for leverage, it is not necessary to short stock and incur interest expense as well as short stock risks.

An uncovered short put occurs when you sell a put. The risk is not the same as that for an uncovered call. With a call, demand can in theory drive a stock's price to unknown levels. But price can only fall so far. This risk is usually thought of as zero; so if you sell a put with a strike price of 25, your maxi-mum exposure is $2,500 minus the premium you receive for selling the put. On a practical level, however, your real short risk is limited to the company's tangible book value per share. It is unlikely that a stock will fall below that level. So if the company's book value is $22 per share and you sell a short put with a strike price of 25, your exposure is three points, or $300. If you receive that much or more for the short put, you elimi-nate the risk. That does not mean you will always avoid exer-cise; it does mean that if the put is exercised and you are required to acquire 100 shares at the strike price, it will be a reasonable price to pay for that stock (even though the price will be lower at the time the put is exercised).

The calculation of return for options is complex whenever stock transactions are involved as well. However, these are impor-tant considerations because options are the most practical method of stock market leverage. Compared to the use of margin accounts, options are also lower-risk strategies if used properly.

The calculation of return on long options, as previously ex-plained, is simple. It requires a calculation of the return based on purchase price; and because options tend to expire in less than one year, it is also necessary to annualize that return (not to create a realistic expectation but to be able to compare transactions). Some options may extend beyond one year, in which case annualizing in equally important. These long-term options, called Long-Term Equity AnticiPation Securities (LEAPS), are written out as far as three years and expire each January.

Returns on covered calls can be calculated without including gains or losses on stock, or combined with stock to view overall return. The selection of a strike price should always be based on your original cost and on tax considerations. You will want to pick a strike price that will produce a net profit in the stock if the call is exercised. You also want to ensure that you will maintain long-term capital gain status when your profit will be substantial, and federal tax rules may remove the long-term status of stock if you write deep in-the-money calls.

The first method for calculating gain on short calls is isolated to calls by themselves. The call may expire worthless, in which case your net profit is 100%; it may be closed before expiration, in which case the net difference between opening sale and closing purchase is a gain or loss; or the short call may be exercised.

Upon exercise, tax rules require that you net the call against the stock basis. For example, you buy 100 shares at $35 and later write a covered call for 40 and receive 4 ($400). The stock rises to $46 per share, and your call is exercised. The combined gain is:

Strike price	$ 4,000
Less: original basis	− 3,500
Gain on stock	$ 500
Plus option premium	400
Total return	$ 900

The return is reported in this manner for federal tax purposes. For your own analysis, it can be treated separately as two different transactions:

1. stock gain ($500 ÷ $3,500 = 14.3%)

2. option gain is 100%

Unfortunately, this method does not provide you with a comparative analysis between two or more different covered call transactions. Furthermore, it excludes dividend income and does not allow for annualized return. To properly create a comparison, you need to calculate the *annualized total return if exercised*. This includes all sources of income and also provides for annualization. The formula:

FORMULA: ANNUALIZED TOTAL RETURN IF EXERCISED

$$\left(\frac{C + O + D}{B} \ (\div \ H) \times 12 \right) = R$$

> *where C = capital gain*
> *O = option premium*
> *D = dividend income*
> *B = original basis in stock*
> *H = holding period in months*
> *R = annualized total return*

For example, if you invest in two different stocks and write covered calls on both, calculating an overall return on the two is the only way to create a realistic comparison. They also need to be annualized in order to make the comparison accurate:

Stock # 1 was purchased at $35 per share 16 months ago. A call with a strike price of 40 was written, and you received $400 in premium. Over the past 16 months, you have also received $64 in dividend income.

Stock # 2 was purchased 42 months ago at $42 per share. When the price rose above $50 per share, you sold a call with a strike price of 50 and received $600. Initial evaluation concluded that your stock capital gain upon exercise would be $800 (strike price of $50 less original cost of $42) plus $600 for the call. The company pays no dividend.

To review both of these transactions in total and on an annualized basis:

Stock # 1

Capital gain on stock	$500
Option premium	400
Dividend income	64
Total income	$964

Holding period 16 months
Basis in stock $3,500

Calculation:

$$\left(\frac{\$964}{\$3,500} \div 16\right) \times 12 = 20.7\%$$

Stock # 2

Capital gain on stock	$800
Option premium	600
Dividend income	0
Total income	$1,400

Holding period 42 months
Basis in stock $4,200

Calculation:

$$\left(\frac{\$1,400}{\$4,200} \div 42\right) \times 12 = 9.5\%$$

The amount of income from stock # 1 was lower that that from stock # 2, but the holding period was shorter, so the annualized return was more than twice as much. This exercise demonstrates two important points. First, the best way to critically compare outcomes for covered calls is through combined return. Second, annualized return is the only way to accurately compare outcomes for stocks with dissimilar holding periods.

Because the stock and option outcomes are really two separate transactions, combining them may be viewed as a distortion of the covered call risk. But realistically, that risk is controlled by you. By selecting a specific strike price, *you* decide the level of capital gain if and when the call is exercised. For example, if your strike price is lower than your basis in the stock, you program in a loss. By choosing to write covered calls only when exercise will create a gain, you eliminate the loss risk. The remaining risk is limited to what would occur if the stock were to rise far above the strike price. Covered call writers accept that risk in recognition of the potentially high returns in covered call writing. Double-digit returns

based on overall stock, option, and dividend income are not difficult to achieve.

The first three chapters focused on calculations of returns
using various methods. These essential calculations form a base for
determining profit or loss; but as the examples of annualized return
calculations have shown, time affects your profits as well as
changes in the dollar value of investments. The following chapter
delves into long-term trends and shows how time works for you or
against you.

CHAPTER 4

Long-Term Trends

Patience Rewarded

THE METHODS BY WHICH RETURNS ARE CALCULATED can be deceiving. When you look at the long-term outcome of an investment, how can you decide whether a particular investment has been better than average or worse? To get the answer, you need to look at compound return on investment over many years.

For example, everyone has heard promotions by mutual funds claiming incredible returns if you had invested $10,000 on a specific date 20 years earlier. You may read that "if you had invested $10,000 exactly 20 years ago, it would be worth more than $26,500 today." As good as this may sound, there are several problems with the claim:

1. *The fund picked a specific date.* If your timing is poor and you invest your $10,000 at a moment when the market is high, it could take many years to recover from a subsequent correction. For example, following the 1929 market crash, it took the market 25 years to recover its losses in a single month. When a mutual fund or other company makes claims about what would have happened to your money, it is able to select a specific date when the market was at a low level.

2. *The outcome is equal to only 5% per year.* The change from $10,000 to more than $26,500 only represents income of 5% per year. This is not an exceptional return at all over a 20-year period. When you consider inflation and taxes in the mix, a 5% return is a net loss after reduced purchasing power is considered.

3. *No consideration is provided for the effect of taxes.* The claims invariably leave out the likely effect of federal and state income taxes. For higher-earning investors, the tax bite is considerable and is likely to affect a decision about where and how to invest.

4. *The fund does not explain its level of fees or charges in the claim.* The claimed outcome might have been a lot higher before the fund deducted its fees. In picking any investment, one of the many comparisons worth making is how much you will be charged per year out of your earnings.

In this chapter, you are provided with methods for calculating a realistic return on your money over many years, whether you invest in stocks, bonds, or mutual funds. The annual return you can get next year might or might not be representative, so evaluation of any investment strategy has to consider the potential for consistent returns year after year. One poor year can wipe out gains for many previous years; so diversifying is wise and reviewing risk levels continually is necessary to prevent losses you cannot afford.

A Realistic View: Long-Term Returns and Annual Rates

There are no definitive or universally agreed upon methods for describing the success of an investment. A friend tells you, "I made a 35% profit on that stock," and this can have several different meanings, including:

• The stock was owned for exactly one year and produced a 35% return.

• The stock was held for 10 years and produced an average annual return of 3.5%.

- The stock was bought on margin, meaning the actual return was greater if based on actual cash invested, but lower because interest expenses were paid as well.

- The transaction was the result of buying a call option, so it was highly leveraged but also probably difficult to repeat.

- Most important of all: This was the one success story in a friend's portfolio, versus a series of disastrous outcomes.

The point to be made about the lack of a definitive way to express outcomes is that you cannot know the whole story from a single statement. It is far more important to know how the entire portfolio performs per year than to know the history of investing in a single stock. You should be dubious about such isolated claims because they are part of a larger outcome; you don't know how long the stock was held or how it was purchased; and even if it was a spectacular success, it would not make sense for you to buy shares today . . . the stock apparently has already produced a 35% return, so the opportunity—if it is accurately portrayed—has passed.

Putting aside the possibility that there is more to the story, you also need to appreciate the difference between a one-time outcome and annual performance. The tendency to focus on the exceptional successes is very human, but it distorts the more important picture of how portfolio performance ends up. The real question should be: *How does your portfolio perform from year to year?*

If you profit by 35% in a single stock but otherwise lose money, it is not a positive outcome. If your *average* portfolio return is only 3% (or a loss of 5%), this is more revealing than what a single stock's price did. The average annual return is the real bottom line of the portfolio. Because annual average returns are going to vary, it is important to calculate outcomes using an average. To calculate an average, add together the number of entries (in this case, rates of return) and then divide the total by the number of periods involved. The formula for *average* is:

FORMULA: AVERAGE

$$\frac{O^1 + O^2 + \ldots O^n}{E} = A$$

> *where O = outcomes*
> *E = number of entries (ⁿ)*
> *A = average*

For example, your portfolio has been in place for six years. Your return on investment (annual profit divided by the year's beginning balance) has been 4.5, 7.0, −1.6, 8.4, 9.3, and −0.7. To compute average for these six years:

$$\frac{4.5 + 7.0 + -1.6 + 8.4 + 9.3 + -0.7}{6} = 4.5\%$$

These rates of return are not atypical; there is no clear pattern or trend; instead, they vary widely from one year to the next. In most individual portfolios, this kind of outcome occurs because of market cycles as well as due to individual decisions concerning investment decisions. Even the timing of a decision may impact overall return dramatically without considering the long-term benefits of a particular investment.

It would not be accurate to tell someone, "I make between 8 and 10 percent return on my portfolio." While that describes two years out of the six, it is far from typical and does not reflect the true average. Another approach, one that reflects the most recent information more than older information, is to use a moving average. For example, you might decide to track your portfolio using the three latest years:

Year	Values in the moving average	Average
3	4.5 + 7.0 + −1.6 (1, 2, and 3)	3.3%
4	7.0 + −1.6 + 8.4 (2, 3, and 4)	4.6
5	−1.6 + 8.4 + 9.3 (3, 4, and 5)	5.4
6	8.4 + 9.3 + −0.7 (4, 5, and 6)	5.7

A comparison between simple average and moving average based on this example is summarized in Figure 4.1.

The moving average may be a more accurate indicator of the portfolio performance in this case. The gradually rising line reflects the most recent three years rather than an ever-larger field of years,

FIGURE 4.1. AVERAGE AND MOVING AVERAGE.

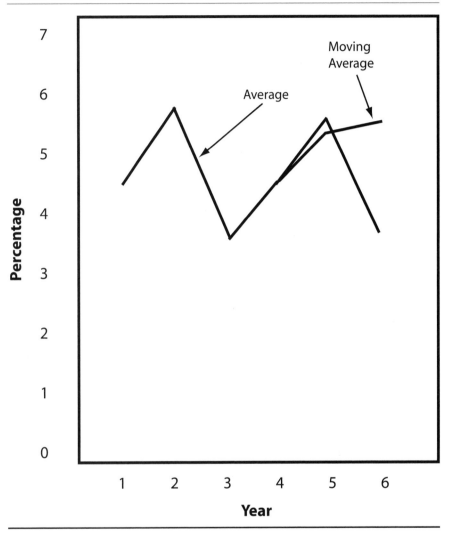

and because the information is perpetually more recent, it has greater reliability.

Using averages to track your portfolio will provide you with an evolving trend over time. It would be inaccurate to focus only on the successful outcomes and to ignore the losses. For example, in any of the six years in the example, you might have had one investment that earned you 12% in only three months. That is a 48% return when annualized. But the obvious fact that you did not make

48% overall that year or in any other year demonstrates that it was not *typical*. Investors—chronically optimistic about the future, but also about parts of the past—do tend to focus on their successes, and that is a positive trait. At the same time, you want to develop and employ a practical and reliable method for judging your portfolio performance.

In the example provided, the moving average grew each year. This trend line should not be expected to move upward relentlessly, but it may indicate that over time, your ability to choose and time investments is improving. That is the kind of conclusion that is valuable in your self-assessment and in any study of your portfolio. You may apply this logic to your own portfolio management or to that provided by a mutual fund, to determine whether your portfolio is succeeding, and to what degree.

Total Net Annualized Return

In previous chapters, some versions of annualized returns have been explained in context. A simple annualized return involved only the basic return on a single transaction; a more complex one involved option premium and dividend payments received. In practice, though, the most accurate study of return on investment should not only be annualized; it should also be expressed net of your tax liability.

This is important for a number of reasons, including:

1. *Tax rates at the state level vary considerably.* It is not realistic to assume a universal return on investment. Every state's tax rules are unique, and there is no uniformity. A few states apply zero income taxes; others tax only investment returns but not ordinary income. So your net annualized return will depend on your state tax rules.

2. *Some investment accounts are not taxable, so results in an IRA account cannot be accurately compared on a pretax level to those in your taxable portfolio.* The calculation of net return will also vary based on the environment where you invest. Thus, if you compare your individual (fully taxable) account to invest-

ment return in your IRA (where taxes are deferred until withdrawal or retirement), you will find a completely different result. An assumed "equal" tax rate won't apply to the IRA either, based on the theory that after retirement your effective tax rate will be lower than today's rate, when you are working full time.

3. *Some investments, such as municipal bonds, are either partially or wholly exempt from income taxes. To compare taxable to nontaxable investments, the tax rate has to be taken into account.* The nature of the investment itself also has to be considered. Certain investments are completely tax-free, others only partially taxable. The comparison between municipal bonds and fully taxable investments has to be made on a net after-tax basis. Many investors discover that they come out slightly ahead with fully taxable investments because (a) the interest rates are higher and (b) the costs are lower. This is especially true if you purchase tax-free bonds through a mutual fund, where costs can be extremely high.

4. *Your individual tax rate changes as income grows and is not identical to after-tax returns earned by other investors.* Even within a single state, your after-tax net return will not be identical to your neighbor's return. As your income increases, so does your tax rate. Deductions and exemptions also affect everyone's tax liability. A family with a mortgage deduction and several children will get more tax breaks than a higher-income working couple with no children and no home mortgage deduction, for example.

The calculation of *net after-tax annualized return* should include both federal and state tax liabilities. For example, if your state's tax rate is 9% and your effective federal rate is 25%, then you will need to use a rate of 34% to figure out your tax. Even though you may be allowed deductions and exemptions that reduce your taxable income, any returns you gain from investment activity should apply the effective tax rate involving both federal and state taxes together. The formula:

FORMULA: NET AFTER-TAX ANNUALIZED RETURN

$$\left(I \times \frac{100 - R}{100} \div M\right) \times 12 = A$$

> where I = income from investments
> R = effective tax rate (federal and state)
> M = months held
> A = net after-tax annualized return

This calculation is complicated by the lower federal rate for long-term capital gains; the exclusion from tax of some types of investments, such as dividends; and great variation in individual state rules. For example, some states tax *only* interest and dividends but not other forms of income.

Assuming that all investment income is subject to the same rules, this formula can be applied as stated. If other forms of income are taxed at lower rates (such as long-term capital gains), those should be excluded from this calculation and calculated separately, and the two separate calculations added together to find the overall return.

When investments are held for different numbers of months, the calculation has to be performed separately for each. This calculation cannot be used for an overall return on your portfolio because annualizing affects the true rate. It has to be applied to each investment, and the purpose of the calculation is to be able to make valid comparisons of outcomes between two or more investments in your portfolio.

You have a lot of control over the net outcome. The tax liability is not going to apply until you close a position, so if your overall income and tax rate were high this year, you can defer selling a stock until the following year, as one example of tax avoidance. You can also time sales of profitable portfolio positions to offset losses in other investments. This helps avoid carrying over losses greater than $3,000 (the annual limitation in capital gains). You can also time the sale of stock or mutual funds to report current-year capital gains when you already have a large carry-over loss to absorb.

▓ Carry-Over Losses and Net Return

When you do apply current-year gains against carry-over losses, it affects your after-tax calculation as well. Because the carry-over loss may in fact reduce your tax liability to zero, the comparison is complex. You will report a zero tax liability on a particular transaction due to the carry-over loss, but next year an identical sale (when no carry-over loss will be available) may well be taxed at a substantial rate.

These variations should always be remembered so that your comparisons will remain valid. Even when you do use a carry-over loss to reduce or eliminate a tax liability, it makes sense to calculate an after-tax return as if you had to pay the tax. In reality, the carry-over loss does not change the effective tax rate; it simply eliminates the tax for the current year. So in order to ensure that your comparisons are valid, your calculation will remain consistent when you apply your effective combined (federal and state) tax rate whether you have to pay it or not.

Because state taxes are computed using different methods and allowing dissimilar deductions than federal, you often end up with a different carry-over number. The federal carry-over may be more or less than the state carry-over. The annual allowance for deduction may be different as well. The carry-over application will distort the actual tax liability, perhaps significantly. But because it applies overall, it is going to be extremely difficult to apply it to any one investment. For example, if your current-year carry-over loss is $4,000 but current-year investment income is $9,000, which specific investments should be assumed to benefit from zero tax? Or should the benefit of the carry-over loss be applied equally to all your investment profits?

Because this carry-over provision applies to your entire investment portfolio and to all your profits in the current year, there is no equitable way to apply the loss. So there is only one possible method to use: Estimate your after-tax profit assuming that there is no carry-over loss. Compare all your profits on the same basis—as they would be taxed without a carry-over—and separate the calculation from the actual outcome.

Some carry-over losses may be significant. Those investors who lost a lot of money in the market of 2001 and 2002 (Enron investors, for example) may never fully absorb their carry-over losses. It is possible that these investors will not have an actual tax liability for many years to come, and perhaps never. But it remains important to compare outcomes between two or more investments on a taxable basis as though no carry-over losses were available, even when none of your investment gains will be taxed this year. Only by using this assumption can you realistically compare investment outcome in your taxable portfolio, your tax-deferred portfolio (an IRA or pension plan, for example), and tax-exempt investments like municipal bonds. If you were to use a zero tax in your computations, it would distort the outcome even when you owe no tax.

This argument also applies when your overall income is lower than your investment profits. For example, if you operate your own business and report a profit each year, your effective tax rate reflects the dollar level of those annual profits. But what happens if your business income is exceptionally low one year? For example, assume your annual return on investments is $15,000 in capital gains, interest, and dividends; and your taxable business income averages $85,000. Your gross income before deductions and exemptions is $100,000. But if your business income next year is only $10,000, your overall gross would be only $25,000. It does not take much in the way of itemized deductions and exemptions to bring your taxable income down to zero.

In this situation, should you use a zero tax rate to compare investments? A valid and realistic comparison of portfolio performance in this situation would not result if you expect the overall gross income level to return to more typical levels the following year. So when you calculate your after-tax returns, it makes the most sense to use a *typical* tax rate rather than the actual rate you will pay this year. The specific circumstances distorting the actual tax liability (carry-over loss or business loss) distort these outcomes and should not be compared to net return in other, more typical years.

The same rationale should be applied in years when your tax rate is exceptionally high. A large profit in your business or in the market can take your federal and state effective tax rates up to the highest brackets, but if those rates are unusual and atypical, it doesn't make sense to compare after-tax returns in those years to after-tax returns in more typical years.

Because of the complexity of tax calculations, attempt to identify a realistic and typical tax rate and apply that to all investment returns, whether you will pay much less or much more in any one year. The comparison should not be distorted by one-time changes in your taxable income. The tax effect cannot be ignored, especially when the overall rate is high, but in years when that rate spikes up or down and away from the average, that typical rate should still be used.

Realistic Expectations: Inflation and Taxes

Taxes alone are not the only factor reducing your net return from investments. Inflation also has to be considered in the mix. One consequence of inflation is reduced purchasing power of your money. In other words, $1.00 today will buy only $0.97 worth of goods after a 3% inflation year.

One of the most important calculations every investor needs to perform is the *breakeven return* they need to earn net of inflation and taxes. In the interest of avoiding risk, if you select investments with returns lower than your breakeven point, you end up losing money on a post-tax, post-inflation basis.

The calculation of breakeven return is:

FORMULA: BREAKEVEN RETURN

$$\frac{I}{100 - R} = B$$

> *where I = rate of inflation*
> *R = effective tax rate (federal and state)*
> *B = breakeven return*

For example, if the current rate of inflation is 3% per year and your effective tax rate (federal and state combined) is 34%, your breakeven return is:

$$\frac{3}{100 - 34} = 4.5\%$$

VALUABLE RESOURCES:

Current inflation rates are provided free of charge at http://inflationdata.com/Inflation/Inflation_Rate/CurrentInflation.asp and also from the Bureau of Labor Statistics at www.bls.gov/cpi.

In other words, you need to earn 4.5% on your money just to break even, considering both taxes and inflation:

Basis invested		$100.00
Assumed gross return, 4.5%	$4.50	
Less: 34% tax	1.53	
Less: Inflation, 3%	3.00	
Total reductions	$4.53	

This example shows that on a "net, net" basis—reducing the 4.5% return for both taxes and inflation—the investment yielded nothing (except −$0.03 due to rounding). To calculate your own breakeven point, use the chart in Table 4.1.

A stark reality is that when both taxes and inflation are taken into account, simply keeping pace with the purchasing power of your capital is a challenge. It makes no sense to select investments that are extremely safe but yield a return below your breakeven; to do so means to lose. At the same time, as the breakeven rises due to the double effect of taxes and inflation, it becomes ever more difficult to consistently achieve a breakeven. To do so requires greater market risks.

These realities about taxes and inflation demonstrate the importance of tax deferral and reinvesting earnings. When you rein-

TABLE 4.1. BREAKEVEN RATES.

Effective tax rate	*I n f l a t i o n R a t e*					
	1%	2%	3%	4%	5%	6%
14%	1.2%	2.3%	3.5%	4.7%	5.8%	7.0%
16%	1.2	2.4	3.6	4.8	6.0	7.1
18%	1.2	2.4	3.7	4.9	6.1	7.3
20%	1.3	2.5	3.8	5.0	6.3	7.5
22%	1.3	2.6	3.8	5.1	6.4	7.7
24%	1.3%	2.6%	3.9%	5.3%	6.6%	7.9%
26%	1.4	2.7	4.1	5.4	6.8	8.1
28%	1.4	2.8	4.2	5.6	6.9	8.3
30%	1.4	2.9	4.3	5.7	7.1	8.6
32%	1.5	2.9	4.4	5.9	7.4	8.8
34%	1.5%	3.0%	4.5%	6.1%	7.6%	9.1%
36%	1.6	3.1	4.7	6.3	7.8	9.4
38%	1.6	3.2	4.8	6.5	8.1	9.7
40%	1.7	3.3	5.0	6.7	8.3	10.0
42%	1.7	3.4	5.2	6.9	8.6	10.3

vest capital gains, interest and dividends, you achieve a compound return on your money.

The effect of inflation and taxes on a single year's return may be a serious reduction in actual profitability. But because compound returns accelerate over time, reinvestment makes sense. Mutual funds allow reinvestment of all forms of income, as an automatic occurrence; other than electing to receive dividends in additional partial shares, you need to take steps on your own to create compound returns. When you create a capital gain by selling stock, for example, you need to figure out how to reinvest those funds as quickly as possible to continue keeping your capital at work. If you time your decisions based on market movements and trends, this may be quite difficult. For example, if you believe you should be out of the market right now, where do you invest your funds?

At the very least, available funds should be kept in a money market account and allowed to earn interest until you select another investment. The importance of compound returns is best understood when you see how the time value of money works. In fact, *time* is the essential element in creating powerful long-term returns by keeping money at work.

▉ Compound Return Calculations

Investors need to track their investments in terms of how their capital is put to work. As a stockholder, you can afford to wait out a slow period in the market. However, if it takes five years for you to realize a 20% return, that is only 4% per year. The time element is an essential ingredient in comparative judgment about the success of an investment program and the effectiveness of your decisions.

This argument applies not only to capital gains and dividends, but also to interest on money market accounts or bond funds. If your bond fund invests in long-term but low-yielding high-grade bonds, it is possible that these "safe" decisions will lag behind your required breakeven return.

Whether applied to interest, dividends, or capital gains, figuring out your annual returns is the most reliable method for comparison. The annualization formula is easily applied to any simple return; but in fact, the stated interest rate can also vary depending on compound methods. When interest is compounded, it means the calculation is performed more than once per year, or that year-to-year interest is added to the principal balance and carried forward. With a compounding effect, you gain an accelerating return over many years. This is why the claim that $10,000 turns into $26,500 over 20 years sounds good, but is dismal. It is only a 5% return, but this is compounded year after year, so an investment earns interest not only on the amount invested, but on accumulated interest as well. This interest on interest (compounding) is what makes the time element so critical.

Compounding methods describe the number of times per year that interest is calculated. For example, when you are told that an investment earns 6%, is this an annual rate without adjustment? Or is the calculation of interest performed semiannually, quarterly, monthly, or daily? These distinctions make a difference in the annual percentage rate (APR) of the investment.

The basic interest computation involves three elements: principal, interest, and time. The formula for *interest* is:

FORMULA: INTEREST

$$P \times R \times T = I$$

where P = principal
R = interest rate
T = time
I = interest

For example, assuming that interest is calculated only once per year, a 6% rate applied to $100 would be:

$100 × 6% × 1 = $6.00

In calculating interest, the stated rate is actually expressed in decimal form; so 6% becomes 0.06. The annual interest is $111 × 0.06, or $6.00 per year.

This process becomes more involved when interest is calculated on a compounded method. For example, if 6% is to apply on a semiannual basis (twice per year), the annual rate is divided by the number of periods and then multiplied twice. The formula for *semiannual compounding* is:

FORMULA: SEMIANNUAL COMPOUNDING

$$(1 + (R \div 2))^2 = I$$

where R = stated interest rate
I = annual percentage rate (APR)

For example, if the $100 deposit is to be compounded semiannually, it should be multiplied by the APR as calculated above:

$$(1 + (0.06 \div 2))^2 = I$$
$$(1 + 0.03)^2 = I$$
$$1.03 \times 1.03 = 1.0609$$

The $100 deposit will grow annually at a rate of 6.09% using semiannual compounding:

$100.00 × 1.0609 = $106.09

The calculation, performed twice per year, provides a simplified version of how compounding works:

1st six months: **$100.00 × 1.03 = $103.00**
2nd six months: **$103.00 × 1.03 = $106.09**

The same process is used for calculation of quarterly compounding. However, there are four periods per year instead of two. The formula for *quarterly compounding* is:

FORMULA: QUARTERLY COMPOUNDING

$$(1 + (R \div 4))^4 = I$$

> *where R = stated interest rate*
> *I = annual percentage rate (APR)*

For example, if the $100 deposit is to be compounded quarterly, it should be multiplied by the APR as calculated above:

$$(1 + (0.06 \div 4))^4 = I$$
$$(1 + 0.015)^4 = I$$
$$1.015 \times 1.015 \times 1.015 \times 1.015 = 1.0614$$

The $100 deposit will grow annually at a rate of 6.14% using quarterly compounding:

$$\$100.00 \times 1.0614 = \$106.14$$

The calculation is performed four times per year:

1st quarter: **$100.00 × 1.015 = $101.50**
2nd quarter: **$101.50 × 1.015 = $103.02**
3rd quarter: **$103.02 × 1.015 = $104.57**
4th quarter: **$104.57 × 1.015 = $106.14**

The process is identical no matter which compounding method is used; only the number of periods varies. So with monthly compounding, there are 12 periods involved. The formula for *monthly compounding* is:

FORMULA: MONTHLY COMPOUNDING

$$(1 + (R \div 12))^{12} = I$$

where R = stated interest rate
I = annual percentage rate (APR)

For example, if the $100 deposit is to be compounded monthly, it should be multiplied by the APR as calculated above:

$$(1 + (0.06 \div 12))^{12} = I$$
$$(1 + 0.005)^{12} = I$$

$1.005 \times 1.005 \times 1.005 \times 1.005 \times 1.005 \times 1.005 \times 1.005 \times 1.005 \times 1.005 \times 1.005 \times 1.005 \times 1.005 = 1.0617$

The $100 deposit will grow annually at a rate of 6.17% using monthly compounding:

$100.00 × 1.0617 = $106.17

The calculation is performed four per year:

1st month:	$100.00 × 1.005 = $100.50
2nd month:	$100.50 × 1.005 = $101.00
3rd month:	$101.00 × 1.005 = $101.50
4th month:	$101.50 × 1.005 = $102.01
5th month:	$102.01 × 1.005 = $102.52
6th month:	$102.52 × 1.005 = $103.03
7th month:	$103.03 × 1.005 = $103.55
8th month:	$103.55 × 1.005 = $104.07
9th month:	$104.07 × 1.005 = $104.59
10th month:	$104.59 × 1.005 = $105.11
11th month:	$105.11 × 1.005 = $105.64
12th month:	$105.64 × 1.005 = $106.17

Finally, interest can also be compounded daily using one of two methods. The actual number of days in the year, or 365, is the first method; or a method often used in banking assumes twelve 30-day months and a 360-day year. The formula for *daily compounding (actual days)* is:

FORMULA: DAILY COMPOUNDING (ACTUAL DAYS)

$$(1 + (R \div 365))^{365} = I$$

where R = stated interest rate
I = annual percentage rate (APR)

The formula for *daily compounding (banking method)* is:

FORMULA: DAILY COMPOUNDING (BANKING METHOD)

$$(1 + (R \div 360))^{360} = I$$

where R = stated interest rate
I = annual percentage rate (APR)

The applications of various rates of compounding depend on the circumstances. If you are paid a quarterly dividend, for example, you would compute your annual return using the quarterly method. For example, if your current yield is 5.5%, the annual compounded interest will be:

$$(1 + (0.055 \div 4))^4 = I$$
$$(1 + 0.01375)^4 = I$$
$$1.01375 \times 1.01375 \times 1.01375 \times 1.01375 = 1.0561$$

Compound interest also works against you. When you owe money, compounding more frequently translates into greater interest. For example, home mortgage debt is usually subject to monthly compounding. Your monthly interest consists of one-twelfth of the annual rate, multiplied by the loan's balance forward. This explains why interest is quite high during the early years of the loan and much smaller in the later years. If your mortgage rate is 6% and you are paying over 30 years, the loan is only one-half paid off during the twenty-first year.

The Time Value of Money—Present Value and Accumulated Value

The calculation of interest over many months or years involves many steps. In comparison, a single annual return is not as complex. For most tasks involving portfolio management, your concern will be a one-year return. Tracked over a period of years, the average annual return is the best indicator of how effectively you manage your capital.

In some circumstances, it is necessary to calculate returns over many years, for tasks beyond the year-to-year analysis of specific investments. For example, if you were to place a specific sum of capital into a fixed-income investment (such as a bond), and if interest were compounded for that entire period, what would the investment be worth after a number of years?

This calculation, called *accumulated value*, reveals how a fixed-interest investment will grow over many periods. The formula:

FORMULA: ACCUMULATED VALUE

$$P (1 + R)^n = A$$

> *where P = principal amount*
> *R = interest rate*
> *n = number of periods*
> *A = accumulated value*

For example, if you assume a 5% per year return on a lump sum investment of $1,000.00 for six years, the formula is:

$1,000.00 $(1 + 0.05)^6 = A$
$1,000.00 $(1.05)^6 = A$

$1,000.00 (1.3401) = $1,340.10

This can be proven by performing the calculations for each year:

Year	Interest	Balance
		$1,000.00
1	$50.00	1,050.00
2	52.50	1,102.50
3	55.13	1,157.63
4	57.88	1,215.51
5	60.78	1,276.29
6	63.81	1,340.10

If the assumption involves compounding and not an annual rate, the formula has to be modified. For example, if the above calculation involved quarterly compounding, the formula would need to be adjusted for 24 periods, each one-quarter of one year. The formula for *accumulated value with compounding* is:

FORMULA: ACCUMULATED VALUE WITH COMPOUNDING

$$\frac{R}{P \ (1 \ + \ (R \ \div \ D))^n = A}$$

> where P = *principal amount*
> R = *interest rate*
> D = *division based on compounding method*
> n = *number of periods*
> A = *accumulated value*

In the example of quarterly compounding, the previous formula is revised to:

$1,000.00 (1 + (0.05 ÷ 4)^{24} = A
$1,000.00 (1.0125)^{24} = A
$1,000.00 (1.3474) = $1,347.40

The calculation of a single amount is easily made, but when you plan on depositing an amount periodically, it becomes more complex. For example, you plan to deposit $1,000.00 per year into a mutual fund account, and you assume your average return will be 5%. In this case, you need to calculate the *accumulated value per period*. The formula is:

FORMULA: ACCUMULATED VALUE PER PERIOD

$$P\left(\frac{((1 + R)^n - 1)}{R}\right) = A$$

where *P* = *principal amount*
R = *interest rate*
n = *number of periods*
A = *accumulated value*

Returning to the previous example, assume 5% per year for six years. However, in this case, $1,000.00 is deposited each year:

$$\$1,000.00 \times \frac{(1 + 0.05)^6 - 1}{0.05} = A$$

$$\$1,000.00 \times \frac{(1.3401) - 1}{0.05} = A$$

$$\$1,000.00 \times \frac{0.3401}{0.05} = A$$

$$\$1,000.00 \times 6.802 = \$6,802.00$$

This can be proven by going through the six-year period and showing how the value grows. The result in the balance column shows the balance at the beginning of each year before interest is calculated:

Year	Deposit	Balance Before Interest	Interest	Balance
1	$1,000.00	$1,000.00	$ 50.00	$1,050.00
2	1,000.00	2,050.00	102.50	2,152.50

3	1,000.00	3,152.50	157.62	3,310.12
4	1,000.00	4,310.12	215.51	4,525.63
5	1,000.00	5,525.63	276.28	5,801.91
6	1,000.00	6,801.91 (rounded = $6,802.00)		

As with the previous calculation, if compounding methods other than the annual rate are assumed, the calculation has to be expanded. With quarterly compounding, for example, you would recalculate on one of two bases: First, you would assume a $1,000.00 deposit at the beginning of the year, subject to four interest calculations. Second, you would use the fractional quarterly interest value *and* assume quarterly deposits at the beginning of each quarter.

Another calculation answers an entirely different question. While accumulated value calculates compound growth of a single deposit or a series of deposits, *present value* is a calculation of what you need to place on deposit to reach a target amount in the future. How much cash do you need to put on deposit today to reach that amount, assuming a number of periods and an annual interest rate? The formula for present value is:

FORMULA: PRESENT VALUE

$$F\left(\frac{1}{(1 + R)^n}\right) = P$$

> where F = *fund value*
> R = *interest rate*
> n = *number of periods*
> P = *present value*

For example, if you want to accumulate $1,000 in six years, assuming 5% per year, you can calculate how much you need to put on deposit today:

$1,000.00 (1 ÷ (1.05)^6) = P
$1,000.00 (1 ÷ 1.3401) = P
$1,000.00 × 0.74621 = $746.21

To prove that this works:

Year	Interest	Balance
		$ 746.21
1	$37.31	783.52
2	39.18	822.70
3	41.14	863.84
4	43.19	907.03
5	45.35	952.38
6	47.62	1,000.00

If you compound interest more than once per year, it will be necessary to calculate fractional interest and use more periods. For example, if the above were formulated with quarterly interest, you would need to go out 24 periods and use 1.25% interest per quarter.

Present value reveals how much you need to deposit to reach a desired outcome in the future. A variation involves making a series of periodic deposits to achieve the same end result. This is called *sinking fund payments*. To calculate, assume the deposit is made at the end of the period, and interest is computed on each period's ending balance. The formula for sinking fund payments is:

FORMULA: SINKING FUND PAYMENTS

$$F\left(\frac{1}{(((1 + R)^n - 1) \div R)}\right) = S$$

> where F = *fund value*
> R = *interest rate*
> n = *number of periods*
> S = *sinking fund payments*

For example, if you need to accumulate $1,000.00 at the end of six years, assuming 5% interest per year, how much do you need to deposit at the end of each year? The answer based on the above formula:

$1,000.00 $(1 \div ((1 + 0.05)^6) - 1) \div 0.05 = S$
$1,000.00 $(1 \div (0.3401 \div 0.05) = S$

$1,000.00 (1 \div 6.802) = S
$1,000.00 \times 0.14702 = $147.02

To prove that this works:

Year	Deposit	Balance Before Interest	Interest	Balance
1	$147.02	$ 147.02	$ 7.35	$154.37
2	147.02	301.39	15.07	316.44
3	147.02	463.48	23.17	486.65
4	147.02	633.67	31.68	665.35
5	147.02	812.37	40.61	852.98
6	147.02	1,000.00		

The sinking fund calculation is complex, but the summary above demonstrates that it produces the desired result. As with all these formulas, interest compounded more than once per year involves fractional rates and more periods. If the above were to be calculated quarterly, you would need 24 periods and a quarterly rate of 1.25%.

Present value and sinking fund calculations identify how much you need to attain a desired deposit amount in the future. Another situation arises when you need to know the amount of deposit required today to fund a future series of withdrawals. For example, you may want to place an amount into a mutual fund account now, with the idea of withdrawing an annual amount later to pay for college expenses, retirement, or other specific goals. This *present value per period* calculation is:

FORMULA: PRESENT VALUE PER PERIOD

$$W\left[\left(1 - \frac{1}{(1 + R)^n}\right) \div R\right] = P$$

> where W = *withdrawals in the future*
> R = *interest rate*
> n = *number of periods*
> P = *present value per period*

In order to be able to take future withdrawals (W), you need to know how much to deposit today (P). For example, if you want to be able to withdraw $1,000.00 per year for six years, assuming 5% per year, how much do you need to deposit today? Applying this question to the formula:

$1,000.00 × [(1 − (1 ÷ (1 + 0.05)⁶)) ÷ 0.05] = P
$1,000.00 × [(1 − (1 ÷ 1.3401)) ÷ 0.05] = P
$1,000.00 × [(1 − (0.74621)) ÷ 0.05] = P
$1,000.00 × [0.25379 ÷ 0.05] = P
$1,000.00 × 5.0758 = $5,075.80

To prove this calculation:

Year	Plus: Interest	Less: Withdrawals	Balance
			$5,075.80
1	$253.79	$1,000.00	4,329.59
2	216.48	1,000.00	3,546.07
3	177.30	1,000.00	2,723.37
4	136.17	1,000.00	1,859.54
5	92.98	1,000.00	952.52
6	47.63	1,000.00	0.15 (rounding)

The deposit made today funds six years' worth of equal withdrawals based on the assumed 5% interest rate. Using compounding methods more frequent than one year requires using the appropriate fractional rate and expanded number of periods.

A final calculation is amortization of a loan. Every homeowner knows that payments consist primarily of interest in the earlier years of a loan and less so as time passes. To calculate the required monthly payment, given the known loan amount, interest rate, and number of years, the formula for *amortization payments* is:

FORMULA: AMORTIZATION PAYMENTS

$$B\left(\frac{1}{V^n}\right) = P$$

where B = balance due on a loan
V = present value per period
n = number of periods
P = payment required

In this formula, the calculated present value per period is based on a known rate. Because the rate is part of another calculation, this abbreviated formula does not include the rate again. To actually calculate the required monthly payment, it is far easier to use one of the many free mortgage calculators online.

VALUABLE RESOURCE:

Search "mortgage calculator" to find numerous free sites. Easy-to-use examples include Web sites for many real estate companies and www.mortgage-calc.com/mortgage/simple.php or http://mortgages.interest.com/content/calculators/monthly-payment.asp.

To figure out an ongoing breakdown between principal and interest, the balance forward is multiplied by the annual rate and divided by 12. This produces the interest portion; the principal is the monthly payment minus interest. The formula for *principal and interest on a monthly payment* is:

FORMULA: PRINCIPAL AND INTEREST ON A MONTHLY PAYMENT

Interest

$$B\left(\frac{R}{12}\right) = I$$

Principal

$$T - I = P$$

New Balance Forward

$$B - P = N$$

> *where B = balance forward*
> *R = annual interest rate*
> *I = interest amount*
> *T = total monthly payment*
> *P = principal*
> *N = new balance forward*

For example, your monthly mortgage payment is $599.55. Your loan balance is $100,000.00, and you are paying a fixed rate of 6%. Applying these formulas:

Interest

$$\$100,000.00 \left(\frac{6\%}{12}\right) = \$500.00$$

Principal

$$\$599.55 - \$500.00 = \$99.55$$

New balance forward

$$\$100,000 - \$99.55 = \$99,900.45$$

Understanding the time value of money is essential to any comparative analysis of a stock portfolio. But even when you are able to track returns over time, you also have to ensure that your raw numbers are accurate. In the next chapter, you will see why it is necessary to adjust the numbers reported by corporations to arrive at the *core* earnings and net worth.

CORE EARNINGS AND NET
WORTH ADJUSTMENTS

MAKING THE NUMBERS REAL

BEFORE EMBARKING ON A DISCUSSION of fundamental analysis (the two chapters that follow), it is important to make a few distinctions between what is reported on financial statements and what is real. If fundamental analysis is to be reliable and accurate, making core earnings adjustments is a necessary first step.

When Standard & Poor's (S&P) Corporation developed its concept of "core earnings," the estimate was that the S&P 500 corporations had earnings overstated by about 30% during the first year the adjustment was calculated.[1] The core earnings (or "true economic profit") of a company may be significantly different from the earnings a company reports under the present system. But what is allowed and what is accurate are not the same, and this is where the problem arises. A 30% downward adjustment obviously not only affects the profitability and equity of a company, but also makes most forms of financially based analysis useless. For this

---

[1] "2002 S&P Core Earnings," *Business Week Online,* October 2002; through June 2002, reported profits for the 500 corporations totaled $26.74 per share versus a core net profit of only $18.48, a reduction of 30%.

reason, using the core net profit and core net worth is a reliable means for applying financial formulas and ratios.

Where do you find these data? Fortunately, S&P calculates the often complex adjustments between reported and core earnings on its Stock Reports service. The reports for each company, including a 10-year financial summary, are provided by some online brokerage services free of charge. Charles Schwab, for example, contains a link for each listed company to the Stock Reports and other analysis services.

The Problem with Today's Accounting Rules

The accounting industry is assumed to be the watchdog of publicly listed companies. Every company trading stock is required to undergo periodic independent audits and produce certified financial statements. For decades, the investing public has viewed this process as its line of defense against fraud and inaccuracy.

The confidence placed in the independent audit is misplaced.

The audit process is not proactive. Many investors assume that the audit is designed to discover and fix problems, but in fact it is a very passive activity. The audit is actually designed to ensure that the accounting decisions conform to GAAP. These standards are complex and at times contradictory, so in practice the audit team will insist on changes only when accounting decisions are glaringly wrong. Even then, there have been numerous instances in which incorrect or even dishonest accounting decisions have not been reversed during an audit. The extreme case of Enron is only one of many instances where corporations have deceived investors and the independent audit has not fixed the problem.

The reasons are many, including:

1. *Basic conflict of interest.* The audit firm doesn't restrict its activities to an annual audit. Most firms also perform numerous consulting tasks for their audit clients, including design of internal systems, legal and personnel work, and accounting functions themselves. This involvement creates two problems. First, the auditing firm often ends up auditing its own work. Second,

revenues from consultation are approximately equal to revenues from auditing. So consulting has become a major source of revenue for the auditing firms. The conflict of interest is glaring. And the legislation passed in 2002 (Sarbanes-Oxley Act) was designed to fix this problem, but it has had little effect.

2. *Close relationships between executives and auditors.* Historically, the audit team worked closely with the CEO and CFO, often negotiating and compromising on proposed changes in accounting policies. If an audit team was too inflexible in its insistence that certain decisions had to be changed, the company might decide to change to another auditing firm. Because auditors are judged within their firm by revenue production, losing a big client could be disastrous for a person's career.

   In addition, many auditors have always been recruited from client ranks, so an accounting executive may easily end up working for the auditing firm. The Sarbanes-Oxley Act (SOX) places restrictions on audit work by anyone working for a client in the recent past, but this situation only limits the degree of the problem. The failure by the accounting industry to maintain distance between itself and its clients is disturbing.

3. *Failure to take the auditing role as a public responsibility.* In theory, the audit is independent and is performed on behalf of the company's shareholders. In practice, executives and the board's audit committee decide which firm to hire (or fire), and the auditing industry has not taken its role seriously. The very idea that the independent audit is designed to protect shareholders from unethical executives has simply not worked. And SOX has not fixed that problem. Several years after the Enron scandal, the financial news consistently reveals corporate financial problems.

4. *A cultural desire to keep stock prices high.* Auditors understand all too well that corporations want their stock price to remain high. A CEO and CFO depend on ever-higher prices to earn their incentive-based compensation. These bonus and option packages often exceed their base pay and represent millions of dollars per year. This creates an obvious conflict for the executives. If earnings fall below expectations this year, the stock

price is likely to fall as well. If a drop of several points in the stock's value represents several million dollars in compensation, it is important. The auditor may not direct or conspire with an executive to artificially inflate earnings, but this cultural aspect of accounting is widely understood. When earnings meet expectations, everyone is happy.

The problems of how the numbers get reported are significant. For anyone depending on audited financial statements to perform an analysis of a corporation, this is a disturbing reality. But the numbers do reveal the truth in many ways. The following guidelines help to get around the deception and inaccuracy of audited financial statements:

1. *Long-term trends reveal the truth.* Studying one year's financial statements does not tell you much at all. You need to (a) identify the ratios you find most useful and (b) look for long-term trends in those ratios. The next two chapters help to reduce the number of possible ratios to a few of the most valuable financial tests to perform over many years.

2. *Using specific formulas in combination reveals hidden facts.* The use of any one ratio reveals part of the picture. But to truly understand what is going on, you need to have all of the pieces. For example, testing working capital by tracking current assets and liabilities (through the current ratio) is instructive, but to see the entire picture, you also need to track long-term debt. Watching revenues over time is also useful, and most investors like to see revenues rise each year. But if profits are flat or falling, the rise in revenues is not useful; so you also need to track expense levels and profits each year.

3. *Inconsistent results are a danger signal.* Investors naturally like predictability in the financial results of companies. When revenues and earnings gyrate wildly from one year to the next, it is impossible to estimate a direction. You often see a corresponding level of volatility in stock prices, so big changes from year to year may indicate that the company is not in control of its

markets and sales; or, even worse, it may indicate that some accounting shenanigans are in practice.

4. *Big changes between reported earnings and core earnings may serve as the most important red flag of all.* When S&P developed its core earnings concept, it provided a valuable service to investors. Core earnings—earnings from a primary product or service and excluding nonrecurring items—are the true picture of corporate performance. This number is easily found in the S&P Stock Reports, which include a 10-year history of key financial results. You will discover that well-managed companies tend to have relatively low core earnings adjustments in most years. (When a company sells off an operating unit, for example, that creates a large core earnings adjustment, but generally speaking, core earnings adjustments should be minor.) You will also discover that companies with low core earnings adjustments tend to report lower than average stock price volatility, and companies with exceptionally high core earnings adjustments tend to reveal higher than average price volatility.

Flaws in the GAAP System—a Passive Approach to Reporting

There is no single, central control of the GAAP system. In fact, it is a loosely organized set of rules, guidelines, and opinions. The two major organizations involved in development of these rules are the Financial Accounting Standards Board (FASB), an independent organization; and the American Institute of Certified Public Accountants (AICPA), the organization overseeing the accounting industry.

VALUABLE RESOURCES:

To find out how the major GAAP organizations function, check their Web sites: www.fasb.org and www.aicpa.org.

The entire GAAP structure is managed by these two organizations, but GAAP includes much more. Publications include high-level interpretations, opinions, and research bulletins; guidelines and statements of position; task force publications and practice bulletins; implementation guides; and issue papers, technical practice aids, pronouncements, and accounting textbooks and articles.

It is fair to say that GAAP consists of all current opinions, observations, and interpretations of how the industry is supposed to work. Change within this complex structure takes time because any proposed new approach is subject to a lengthy review process on several levels. As you might expect, within such a highly technical but loosely organized structure, many different opinions exist and justification for a particular interpretation may easily be found. So in spite of its public image, the accounting and auditing industry is far from specific in its determinations. When a senior auditor confronts a decision that seems to not conform to GAAP, discussions with the company's financial employees may result in (a) a change in the financial outcome, (b) modification of the transaction, or (c) no change whatsoever. It all depends on how aggressively the auditor wants to take a stand and whether or not some justification can be found in the vast publication arena of GAAP.

Because auditors have a well-known conflict of interest in working on both audits and consultation projects for the same companies, SOX attempted to inhibit some of the more egregious problems in five ways:

1. It set up a Public Company Accounting Oversight Board (PCAOB) to supervise firm practices and, if necessary, to impose sanctions. The board is a private sector, nonprofit organization, but it reports to the Securities and Exchange Commission (SEC). However, the effectiveness of this oversight board is difficult to judge. In its first five years of existence, no major sanctions have been imposed against any of the large national accounting firms. The PCAOB did issue 2003 reports on its examinations of the four major accounting firms, which provide some general guidelines for accounting interpretations.

VALUABLE RESOURCES:

Check the work of the SEC and PCAOB by visiting their Web sites: www.sec.gov and www.pcaobus.org.

2. Non-audit services were restricted. SOX named many services that auditing firms were no longer allowed to provide for those companies for which auditing work is also performed. However, this provision has not affected accounting firms' ability to generate non-audit revenues. In fact, there is no apparent reduction in revenues among any of the large accounting firms since SOX was enacted. Within the first year following SOX, the Big Four firms continued reporting between $3 and $5 billion per year in non-audit revenues.[2]

3. Auditors have to rotate off accounts. In the past, senior auditors were fixtures in the offices of larger clients. Maintaining objectivity is impossible when people become so familiar with those being audited. SOX requires partners to rotate off accounts within a five-year period.

4. Auditors report to the audit committee, not to financial executives. Before SOX, auditors met regularly with the CEO or CFO and negotiated changes to accounting decisions. This led to many problems, not the least of which was loss of objectivity for auditors themselves. Executives made decisions to hire or fire firms, giving them tremendous control. Now, though, the board's audit committee makes those decisions and meets with auditors directly.

5. Auditors cannot move into positions with a client's company. In the past, companies hired financial executives from the audit team directly, so that the current year's audit was conducted with a recent employee of the accounting firm itself. Under SOX, the auditing firm cannot conduct an audit for any company that has hired a member of senior management from that firm within the past year.

[2] Cassell Bryan-Low, "Accounting Firms Are Still Consulting," *Wall Street Journal*, September 23, 2002.

Have these provisions fixed the problems? They have not. There remains a widespread cultural attitude in the accounting industry that views past compliance problems as matters of public relations rather than as serious internal flaws. This means that in order to be able to rely on financial statements, you cannot simply accept a certification from an "independent" auditing firm as the last word. Real independence remains elusive. So in calculating the valuation and profitability of a company, you need to be able to isolate noncore earnings and make adjustments on your own. S&P's Stock Reports summarize the core earnings numbers, which helps considerably by providing reliable numbers. But going beyond the one-line identification of *core earnings*, it is also necessary to look critically at (a) the level of adjustments a company needs each year and the trend in that adjustment, (b) the degree of disclosure and explanation the company provides, and (c) efforts to achieve real transparency.

It is clear that the accounting industry has no interest in true reform of its practices. It is up to corporations to make meaningful change. For example, it would be simple for corporations to rule that they will not use their auditing firm for any non-audit work. This may cause a few short-term problems, but it would certainly send the message to the investing public that corporate management is serious about fixing its own problems.

Examples of Material Expenses

A core earnings adjustment is necessary when any *material* expense is improperly excluded from the list of expenses; or when any *material* revenue is included, but it is a one-time event. "Material" simply means that the dollar value of the transaction makes a difference in the outcome of the financial report (the valuation of the company as reported on its balance sheet or the earnings as reported on its operating statement).

Typically, material expenses that may be left off the GAAP-approved operating statement include:

Stock options granted to executive or employees. The stock option is a form of compensation, but under traditional accounting rules, the value of these options was never reported as an expense—even though their value could be huge. So the expense simply vanished and investors had no idea how much compensation executives earned if and when they cashed in their options. Because stockholders have to pay for those options out of the company's assets, the effect is very real even though it did not show up anywhere. The large dollar value of stock options has led some companies to voluntarily report the expense, and others to do away with options altogether. Gradually, the system is reforming, and stock option expense is showing up in some instances.

Contingent liabilities. Many companies *might* owe a great deal of money to others, but the contingent expense is not shown on the operating statement. For example, two very large companies—Merck and Altria—face thousands of lawsuits and may owe great sums of money in the future to settle those suits. Merck's Vioxx-related problems and the ongoing problems for Altria relating to tobacco lawsuits could come out to very large expenses in future years. But contingent liabilities are summarized in footnotes and not on the operating statement. Under the GAAP rules, expenses are supposed to be shown in the year incurred, so realistically the expense of losing a lawsuit cannot be recorded until the loss occurs. However, it would make sense for companies to set up loss reserves as liabilities and record an annual expense in anticipation of future litigation losses—especially when those potential losses will be large. A formula similar to that used to set up bad debt reserves would mitigate this problem.

Core earnings can also go the other way. Companies may include revenue that will not recur; as a result, these items should be removed from the operating statement:

Capital gains from the sale of assets. When companies sell off assets, they book the revenue; however, this is a nonrecurring form of revenue and will not recur in the future in the same way that core revenue would be expected to recur. Capital gains are usually listed below the operating net earnings as a form of "other income," but the question should be raised as to whether the earnings per share (EPS) includes capital gains. If it does, then the EPS is inaccurate.

Revenue from selling operating segments. Companies also may sell off operating segments. For example, a few years ago Altria sold its Miller Brewing segment and booked $2.6 billion revenue from the sale. But this was noncore revenue because it was not profit derived from recurring sales of product. In any study of revenue and earnings for Altria, you would need to restate earnings to (a) remove the nonrecurring earnings and (b) also remove Miller Brewing revenues from previous years to accurately track remaining revenues into the future.

Revenue from nonrecurring accounting changes. Companies make technical changes in the way they value some of their assets. For example, calculating bad debt reserves or setting valuation of inventory may be changed, affecting earnings during the year the change goes into effect. This is a noncore adjustment and should be removed from the core earnings.

Altering the reported outcome on the operating statement does not negate the transactions. For example, when a company is paid for selling an operating unit, the money is very real. But under core earnings adjustments, these items have to be excluded in order to estimate any trends and to judge how growth is likely to occur in the future. Noncore items distort this analysis; so before embarking on development of any fundamental trends, these core earnings adjustments have to be made.

Balance Sheet Problems—Inaccurate Valuation

Adjusting core earnings is only half of the picture. When revenues and earnings are distorted by noncore transactions, the balance sheet—where assets, liabilities, and net worth are reported—is also altered as a consequence.

It is often shocking for investors to learn that some very large liabilities are routinely excluded from the balance sheet. In fact, the balance sheet does not provide an accurate summary of assets, liabilities, or net worth. The accounting standards applied to how these items are valued fall short of what investors should expect. Some examples:

Pension liabilities. The ever-growing pension liabilities of many large corporations are not reported anywhere. GM owes billions in its pension liability, and rumors have begun that the company (or at least its pension plan) may be bankrupt. Similar problems have been disclosed by many airlines and other companies in recent years.

Long-term lease obligations. Many corporations enter into long-term leases for their plant or equipment, often going out 30 years or more. These obligations show up from year to year as current expenses, but the contractual obligations—very tangible liabilities—are not shown in the list of corporate liabilities, and this reporting is not required under GAAP rules.

Contingent liabilities. Just as expenses may be understated due to contingent liabilities, the liabilities themselves are not reported anywhere except in a footnote of the annual report. In those cases where the contingent liability could be significant, companies should set up a reserve in the liability section and add to it each year, but under GAAP this is not required.

Stock option liability. Stock options granted to executives and employees in past years remain as obligations of the corporation. If those options are exercised, the employee is able to purchase stock below current market value. This dilutes the value of stock for the remaining stockholders, especially since many such transactions involve purchases of stock at the option price and an immediate sale at market price. That difference is an expense to the company, and the liability does not show up anywhere on the balance sheet.

Asset valuation. Just as liabilities are understated, assets may be as well. Under GAAP rules, depreciable assets are always booked at purchase price and depreciated over a number of years. So while land values on the balance sheet remain the same as the original purchase price, the value of buildings and other improvements declines each year until their book value is zero. It is commonplace for corporations to own vast holdings of real estate with little or no book value. As a result, GAAP requires these assets to be treated like equipment and vehicles, which do truly lose value. Real estate usually appreciates, so under GAAP rules, the asset section of the balance sheet is often far below true market value, and the real estimated value is reported only in a footnote.

The solution to these material problems in GAAP is to reform the system, but that would take many years. In order for investors to gain a true picture of the companies whose stock they own, true transparency would require a recalculation of asset, liability, and net worth values; and operating statement revenue and earnings. Companies could easily summarize their results in two columns. First would be the GAAP-based outcome you see currently; second would be the core valuation (balance sheet) and core earnings (operating statement).

A true and sincere reform within the accounting industry could (and should) require this disclosure by all publicly listed corporations. But it is not likely that the accounting industry will take any such stand. The reaction of the industry to the revelations of its own complicity in misleading audits throughout the 1990s and into 2001 have made it clear that any real reform in audit standards will have to be imposed and enforced from outside of the accounting industry.

Recalculating the Key Ratios

The importance of core earnings and core valuation adjustments cannot be emphasized too much. In many instances, these adjustments radically change the outlook for corporations. For example, why would anyone invest in GM stock if a true report revealed that the company had no net worth? The answer is obvious: In spite of what the true numbers reveal, the Wall Street culture does not want to face the facts. The auditing industry, Wall Street analysts, bro-

kerage firms, institutional investor management, and corporate executives themselves do not want to reform the system; they do not
want people to realize how poorly the numbers are reported, and
they fear that the entire investment structure would collapse if obvious flaws were corrected all at once. S&P's revelation in 2002 that
the S&P 500 was overvalued by 30% (based on initial core earnings
adjustments) is disastrous. But in fact, investors would make better
decisions with better information.

Until reform occurs, investors need to continue performing
their own fundamental analysis, but with accurately adjusted valuation. When you determine a number of important ratios, both core
earnings and core valuation questions have to be addressed, especially when those adjustments are large. For example, *earnings per
share (EPS)* is considered a key ratio and is widely used as a means
for judging the value of a stock. The formula for this is:

FORMULA: EARNINGS PER SHARE

$$\frac{N}{S} = E$$

> *where N = net earnings*
> *S = shares outstanding*
> *E = earnings per share*

The shares outstanding are computed as an average throughout the
year (compared to earnings for the entire year). For example, if a
company reports 5.218 million shares and its latest year's earnings
were $1.185 million, then EPS would be:

$$\frac{\$1.185}{5.218} = \$0.23$$

However, the EPS calculation is based on *reported* earnings per
share. If the core earnings are considerably lower, then the EPS is
distorted. For example, consider the effect on this calculation if
core earnings were $0.202 million:

$$\frac{\$0.202}{5.218} = \$0.04$$

The difference between $0.23 per share EPS and $0.04 is considerable. This is not an exaggerated example. It is based on the 2005 results for Lucent Technologies (LU). The calculation of *core earnings per share (CEPS)* is:

FORMULA: CORE EARNINGS PER SHARE

$$\frac{N + (-) A}{S} = C$$

where N = net earnings
A = core earnings adjustments
S = shares outstanding
C = core earnings per share

The adjustments may increase or decrease the reported net earnings. A summary of the reported and core earnings for three companies is shown for four years in Table 5.1.

These comparisons make the point that the difference between EPS and CEPS can be substantial. For example, someone considering a purchase of Lucent Technologies shares might review EPS and conclude that the company has consistently produced profitable results. But when the core numbers are studied, the picture is far more dismal. GM reported *higher* core earnings for three out of the four years shown; in this example, the adjustment for CEPS moves in the opposite direction. IBM was more consistent in the latest three years, with a one-time large core earnings adjustment in 2002. In all cases, the changes between reported and core earnings were important enough to change the analysis.

Two additional ratios should also be adjusted to ensure the accuracy of fundamental analysis. The debt ratio is among the most important tests of a company's ability to maintain a balance between equity and debt. But what about unreported liabilities? For example, GM's reported common equity at the end of 2005 was

TABLE 5.1. REPORTED AND CORE EARNINGS.

	In Millions				
	Net Earnings				
	Reported	*Core*	*Shares*	*EPS*	*CEPS*
Lucent Technologies					
2005	$ 1,185	$ 202	5,218	$ 0.23	$ 0.04
2004	2,002	754	5,313	0.38	0.14
2003	770	(1,980)	3,950	0.19	(0.50)
2002	1,826	(16,627)	3,426	0.53	(4.85)
General Motors					
2005	$(10,458)	$(6,741)	565	$(18.50)	$(11.93)
2004	2,805	4,040	567	4.95	7.13
2003	2,862	4,510	569	5.03	7.93
2002	1,736	(838)	562	3.09	(1.49)
IBM					
2005	$ 7,994	$ 6,395	1,628	$ 4.91	$ 3.93
2004	8,448	6,923	1,709	4.94	4.05
2003	7,613	5,270	1,756	4.34	3.00
2002	5,334	111	1,731	3.08	0.

Source: Standard & Poor's Stock Reports.

$14.597 billion; but its *unrecorded* pension liabilities were about $37 billion. If you compute the effect of this, GM's negative net worth was over $22 billion.[3] This certainly affects the debt ratio, in fact throwing the calculation into complete disarray. GM's reported debt ratio at the end of 2005 was 91%, the latest entry in a growing negative trend. (The years 2001 through 2005 showed the ratio growing from 79% to 91%, increasing every year.) The "core net worth" of GM is obviously negative if those pension liabilities are to be counted. In recalculating the debt ratio, you need to recalculate net worth for net valuation adjustments. In the case of GM, the ratio cannot be calculated because net worth is negative. To recalculate the debt ratio to the *core debt ratio*, make adjustments to total capitalization (which consists of net worth and long-term debt):

[3] GM reported in 2005 a total of $9 billion in pension liabilities plus an additional $28 billion for "other postretirement pensions." Source: General Motors 10-K filings.

$$\frac{L}{T + (-) A} = C$$

> *where L = long-term debt*
> *T = total capitalization*
> *A = core valuation adjustments*
> *C = core debt ratio*

The extreme case of GM demonstrates that even the reported 91% debt ratio is far from accurate. It is actually well over 100%. Calculations to reflect debt ratio accurately are especially important in those instances where large unreported liabilities will dramatically change the picture.

The same is true for the P/E ratio. This is calculated by dividing the current price per share of stock by the EPS. But recall the dramatic difference between EPS and CEPS in many instances. The fact, for example, that GM has not shown its ever-growing pension liabilities on its balance sheet is a huge problem for the company and for its shareholders. The estimated $37 billion GM reported to the SEC in 2005 may even be understated. According to some calculations, the real post-retirement obligation at the end of 2005 was about $57 billion rather than the $28 billion GM reported. This is based on a reported $20 billion in assets versus $77 billion in obligations in the pension plan.[4]

These off-balance sheet liabilities affect virtually all ratios you would perform in trying to place any kind of value on the stock of GM or any other company with such large adjustments. It brings into question the calculation of earnings as well. Since pension liabilities represent rather large annual expenses to the company— which also remain unreported on the company's operating statement—the P/E ratio is inaccurate as well. Numerous adjustments in earnings (see previously discussed table for three well-known

---

[4] GM's reported numbers, summarized in Allen Sloan, "General Motors Getting Eaten Alive by a Free Lunch," *Washington Post*, April 19, 2005.

stocks) further affect the earnings used in the P/E. To calculate the *core P/E ratio*:

$$\frac{P}{E + (-)\,A} = C$$

where P = price per share
E = earnings per share as reported
A = core earnings adjustments
C = core P/E ratio

In the case of companies like Lucent Technologies and GM, the changes in P/E due to recalculated earnings can be disastrous. Any ratio—including the P/E—is only as valuable as the information used. If P/E is to be used to estimate future trends in stock and corporate value, the core P/E should be the ratio of choice.

Finding Core Earnings—Comparative Analysis

The detailed calculation of core earnings becomes quite technical when all of its aspects are explored. An online search on the subject of core earnings is not especially helpful, and there are no services or shortcuts in making the calculations.

S&P originally developed this system of adjustments as part of its effort to accurately rate bonds issued by listed companies. It continues to emphasize credit ratings on its own Web site. However, the S&P Stock Reports provide a one-line annual summary of net earnings and core net earnings, and this is the most valuable source for finding the number. They are also free with some online brokerage services.

Hopefully, as the mood for accounting reform moves forward, corporations will take the lead in disclosure along with transparency, voluntarily showing core-adjusted earnings as part of their report to investors. S&P would provide a valuable service to investors by expanding its core reporting to include estimates of core

valuation. That would include adjustments for off-balance sheet liabilities like pension obligations; employee stock option debt; the
current and long-term liability for lease commitments; and a re-
serve-calculated expense and approximation of the value of contingent liabilities. On its Stock Reports, further breakdowns of key
ratios (like the debt ratio, current ratio, EPS, and P/E) could also
be provided on two levels: GAAP and core.

All these changes would be valuable to any investor who wants
to track the fundamentals accurately. Without core earnings adjustments, it is virtually impossible to make reliable comparisons
between companies, even when they are in the same industry. For
example, within the retail sector, a review of three leading companies shows how difficult it is to make comparisons without core
earnings adjustments. Table 5.2 shows these results for Wal-Mart,
Federated Department Stores, and Sears Holding Corporation.

These differences between three companies in the same market
sector explain why core earnings adjustments are essential. Wal-

TABLE 5.2. RETAIL CORE EARNINGS ADJUSTMENTS.

	In Millions			
	Net Earnings			
	Reported	*Core*	*Difference*	*%*
Wal-Mart				
2006	$11,231	$ 11,134	$ (97)	−0.9%
2005	10,267	10,267	0	0
2004	8,861	8,861	0	0
2003	8,039	7,955	(84)	−1.0
Federated Department Stores				
2006	$ 1,373	$ 967	(406)	−29.6%
2005	689	655	(34)	−4.9
2004	693	628	(65)	−9.4
2003	638	490	(148)	−22.8
Sears Holding Corporation				
2006	$ 948	$ 696	$(252)	−26.6%
2005	1,106	448	(658)	−59.5
2004	248	(405)	(653)	−263.3
2003	(3,262)	(3,439)	(177)	−5.4

Source: Standard & Poor's Stock Reports.

Mart has a consistent record of virtually no core earnings adjustments; Federated has reported differences that are significant; and Sears has reported net earnings substantially different from its core earnings.

You will not always find such glaring discrepancies within a single industry. But the chances are that the numbers you rely upon—the *same* numbers certified by an independent audit—may, in fact, be highly inaccurate. With this information as a premise for beginning your program of fundamental analysis, the next two chapters provide explanations for the major tests worth using on the balance sheet and on the operating statement of a company.

FUNDAMENTALS

BALANCE SHEET TESTS YOU NEED TO KNOW

THE "FUNDAMENTALS" SIMPLY MEANS THE FINANCIAL INFORMATION a company reports. In the last chapter, the discussion of core earnings demonstrated that the official GAAP version of accounting is unreliable and often distorts the picture completely.

In this chapter, the balance sheet ratios and formulas are examined, and, in the next chapter, you will find the same information for the fundamentals on the company's operating statement.

■ The Nature of Fundamental Analysis

The fundamentals, everyone should remember, are nothing more than a financial history of a company. It is not necessarily the whole truth, or even a complete picture; financial statements at their very best only conform to the standards of GAAP. This means that they may be quite unreliable as a means for judging a company's value. Keep in mind a few essential points concerning fundamental analysis:

1. *All analysis is meant only to improve your estimation; nothing ensures success.* The purpose in studying the numbers is that

they reveal trends. They show clearly what has occurred in the past, which gives you some fairly reliable ideas about how the future might shape up. But there are no guarantees. A "best estimate" is worthwhile, however. Consider a comparison of 10 years' revenue between Wal-Mart and J.C. Penney:[1]

	Revenues (in $millions)	
Year	Wal-Mart	J.C. Penney
2006	$312,427	$18,781
2005	285,222	18,424
2004	256,329	17,786
2003	244,524	32,347
2002	217,799	32,004

This historical summary of revenues demonstrates that while Wal-Mart's growth is consistent and predictable, J.C. Penney's revenues show an inconsistent trend. So if you were to use past information to estimate future revenues and earnings, it would be far easier based on Wal-Mart's fundamentals than on J.C. Penney's.

2. *The fundamentals are always historical, so be aware of the potential for change between the latest report and today's situation.* Whenever you study a financial statement, you have a time problem. It takes quite a while to audit a company's books and to produce a final version of the statements. So from the cutoff date of the statements, it is quite likely that a final report will not be available for at least two months. A lot can happen in that time. For example, if the company closes its books at the end of its highest-volume quarter and you are reviewing results two to three months later, the quarterly results you are looking at are (a) out of date and (b) not accurate for judging the current level of revenue and earnings.

3. *No single indicator should be used alone; the best analysis gathers data from many sources.* Virtually every fundamental indicator has to be reviewed in conjunction with other indicators. For example, tracking revenues alone is not enough; you also need

[1] Wal-Mart and J.C. Penney annual reports.

to track earnings. Returning to the example of comparisons between Wal-Mart and J.C. Penney, a five-year summary of earnings and core earnings is useful along with the revenue trend:[2]

	Earnings (in $millions)			
	Wal-Mart		J.C. Penney	
Year	Reported	Core	Reported	Core
2006	$11,231	$11,134	$977	$960
2005	10,267	10,267	667	662
2004	8,861	8,861	345	345
2003	8,039	7,955	371	171
2002	6,671	6,692	114	41

By the same argument, watching working capital also requires that the capitalization tests be followed closely. Well-informed investors never depend on any single ratio or formula; they review a series of valuable tests together. This does not mean you need to perform dozens of tests, but a few important indicators can reveal a lot.

4. *Before drawing conclusions from a published financial statement, check the difference between reported earnings and core earnings.* As the example above shows, there may be important differences between reported earnings and core earnings. These differences will affect all ratios. In the retail sector, these adjustments have not been historically significant. But in many other sectors, they have been enormous. For example, when S&P first began publishing its core earnings adjustments, many corporations had adjustments in the billions of dollars. These were:[3]

	2002 Earnings (in $millions)		
Company	Reported	Core	Difference
Boeing	$ 2,107.0	$ − 315.5	$ − 2,422.5
Citicorp	15,930.0	13,708.8	− 2,221.2
Du Pont de Nemours	5,069.0	− 346.6	− 5,415.6
ExxonMobil	10,590.0	9,527.0	− 1,063.0

[2] Wal-Mart and J.C. Penney annual reports; and Standard & Poor's Stock Reports.
[3] *Business Week Online*, 2002 index as reported by Standard & Poor's Corporation.

Ford Motor Co.	−5,297.0	−8,412.7	−3,115.7
General Electric	15,158.0	11,225.4	−3,932.6
General Motors	1,829.0	−2,363.5	−4,192.5
IBM	5,657.0	287.3	−5,369.7
Lockheed Martin	378.0	−682.8	−1,060.8
Procter & Gamble	4,228.0	2,870.2	−1,357.8
SBC Communications	6,872.0	4,107.6	−2,764.4

These adjustments, all more than a billion dollars, show that virtually no fundamental analysis can be accurate based on the GAAP-approved methods of reporting. Adjustments for both Du Pont de Nemours and IBM were over $5 billion in that first year that core earnings calculations were performed. Without those adjustments, investors were expected to simply accept the numbers as reported (and still are expected to do so today). So any earnings values used in calculating ratios based on financial reports should be based on core earnings and not on reported earnings.

Basics of the Balance Sheet

The balance sheet is the proper starting point in fundamental analysis. This financial report is so-called because it reports the balances of all asset, liability, and net worth accounts on a specific date. (This date is the same date as the end of the quarter or year reported on the operating statement.) In addition, the sum of all assets must equal the sum of liabilities plus net worth. This is accomplished by the fact that in the double-entry system, every transaction contains a debit and a credit, so that the sum of all entries is always zero. At the end of a reporting period, the profit or loss is "closed" and the value transferred to net worth. This account, retained earnings, becomes a part of the shareholders' equity. Figure 6.1 summarizes the features of the balance sheet.

The figure demonstrates how the balance sheet appears in summarized form. Each account's balance is listed as a single value as of the date of the financial report.

Current assets are those assets in the form of cash or readily convertible to cash within 12 months (cash, accounts receivable, notes receivable, marketable securities, inventory).

FIGURE 6.1. BALANCE SHEET.

Assets	
Current Assets	xxx
Long-Term Assets	xxx
Other Assets	xxx
Total Assets	xxx
Liabilities	
Current Liabilities	xxx
Long-Term Liabilities	xxx
Total Liabilities	
Net Worth	
Capital Stock	xxx
Retained Earnings	xxx
Total Net Worth	xxx
Total Liabilities and Net Worth	xxx

same dollar value

Long-term assets are the capital assets of the company, net of accumulated depreciation (real estate, vehicles, machinery, and equipment).

Other assets include any tangible or intangible assets not included in the other categories (prepaid or deferred assets and intangibles, such as goodwill).

Current liabilities are all debts payable within 12 months, including 12 months' payments on notes and contracts.

Long-term liabilities are all liabilities payable beyond the next 12 months (notes and bonds).

Capital stock is the issued value of all outstanding shares of stock (common and preferred stock).

Retained earnings are the accumulated net earnings or losses during each year.

The balance sheet is the source for many important ratios. Working capital is tested from balance sheet accounts. By definition, working capital is the net difference between current assets and current liabilities. The trend in working capital is among the most important fundamental tests; a company that cannot maintain healthy working capital cannot pay its bills or finance its own growth.

Another important area to test on the balance sheet is trends in capitalization. A corporation funds its operations through equity (capital stock) and debt (notes and long-term bonds). The higher the debt, the greater the future burden on operations. Not only do these debts have to be repaid, but interest has to be paid to debtors as well. The greater the percentage of debt as part of total capitalization, the more profits have to be paid out in interest. This means that as debt rises, less profit remains for future growth or to pay dividends. An exceptionally high debt ratio is a sign of trouble. And if the debt ratio is rising each year, that means the problems are getting worse.

There is often a direct correlation between ever-growing debt levels and core earnings adjustments. A study of the S&P Reports for corporations like GM, Ford, and Lucent makes this point. All have substantial volatility in reported earnings and large annual core earnings adjustments; and all three reported large debt as a percentage of total capitalization:[4]

| | Percentage of Debt to Total Capitalization | | |
Year	General Motors	Ford	Lucent
2005	91%	83%	93%
2004	86	82	130
2003	85	88	252
2002	89	88	258
2001	79	87	20

The *trend* in all these instances is the key. GM reports a steadily rising debt level and 91% of total capitalization in the form of debt. Ford's debt is declining but remains at 83% as of 2005. Lucent's case is problematical for any analyst. How (and why) did the debt level go from 20% to 258% of total capitalization in one year? Any year in which debt is more than 100% reveals that equity is, in fact, negative. The decline to 93% by 2005 is a positive trend, but 93% is exceptionally high. Only 7% of capitalization is held by shareholders. In addition, the wild swings in the debt ratio raise suspicions about the accounting practices and reporting at Lucent. A review of other trends in the company confirms the suspicion because most important ratios have been erratic. And the trend overall for Lucent is negative.

Working Capital Tests

A few important working capital tests help you to identify growth potential (or emerging problems) on the balance sheet. As with all ratio analysis, it is the trend that counts and not only the latest ratio itself. You want to find companies that consistently maintain working capital at an acceptable level.

The first of these is the *current ratio*, a comparison between the balances of current assets and current liabilities. To calculate current ratio, divide current assets by current liabilities:

[4] General Motors, Ford, and Lucent Technologies annual reports.

$$\frac{A}{L} = R$$

> *where A = current assets*
> *L = current liabilities*
> *R = current ratio*

The ratio is expressed as a single digit. For example, if assets are $20 million and liabilities are $10 million, the current ratio is 2:

$$\frac{\$20}{\$10} = 2$$

A popular standard for current ratio is "2 or better." You would expect to see a consistent ratio at or above 2 based on this standard. But the current ratio is a limited indicator. In many very well-capitalized and well-managed companies, a current ratio of 1 is acceptable as long as the dollar values of current assets are strong and earnings are consistent. For example, a five-year summary of the current ratio for Altria and Merck demonstrates that well-managed companies can do well with a current ratio lower than 2:[5]

	Current Ratio	
Year	Altria	Merck
2005	1.0	1.6
2004	1.1	1.1
2003	1.0	1.2
2002	0.9	1.2
2001	0.9	1.1

There may be a trend in both of these cases, but any change is very subtle. A more important trend when it comes to working capital is consistency. In both of these corporations, the relationship between

[5] Altria and Merck annual reports.

current assets and current liabilities has remained consistent. You do not see wide disparity from one year to the next. This controlled fundamental volatility is a positive sign.

A closely related ratio is the *quick assets ratio* (also called the acid test). This is a variation on the current ratio that excludes inventory values. To compute the quick assets ratio:

FORMULA: QUICK ASSETS RATIO

$$\frac{A - I}{L} = R$$

> *where A = current assets*
> *I = inventory*
> *L = current liabilities*
> *R = quick assets ratio*

The acceptable standard for the quick assets ratio is 1. You expect to see consistent ratios reporting equality between current assets and current liabilities. The distinction between current ratio and quick assets ratio becomes significant in industries with large or widely fluctuating inventory levels, especially those where inventory levels change frequently through the year due to sales cycles. This makes quarterly review of the current ratio difficult and year-end review unreliable in some instances. When this is the case, the quick assets ratio may provide a better tracking history.

The most conservative test of working capital is the *cash ratio*. This tests the highly liquid asset relationship to current obligations. The formula:

FORMULA: CASH RATIO

$$\frac{C + M}{L} = R$$

> *where C = cash*
> *M = marketable securities*

$$L = \textit{current liabilities}$$
$$R = \textit{cash ratio}$$

This ratio demonstrates the highest level of liquidity. Cash and marketable securities are immediately available to pay off debts. As the ratio declines or approaches the "1" level, working capital becomes a growing concern. A company should be able to manage its current debts easily from its liquid assets.

The last in this group of ratios is *working capital turnover*. This is an average of the number of times per year working capital is replaced. In accounting, this concept is often used. However, it does not mean that the actual assets and liabilities are eliminated and replaced; it is an estimate based on comparisons between balances. The formula is:

FORMULA: WORKING CAPITAL TURNOVER

$$\frac{R}{A - L} = T$$

$$\textit{where } R = \textit{one year's revenue}$$
$$A = \textit{current assets}$$
$$L = \textit{current liabilities}$$
$$T = \textit{working capital turnover}$$

The result is expressed as a number representing the number of "turns." For example, at the end of the year, a company reported $27.5 billion in revenue; current assets of $4.4 billion; and current liabilities of $2.6 billion. The working capital turnover is:

$$\frac{\$27.5}{\$4.4 - \$2.6} = 15.3 \textbf{ turns}$$

This reveals that working capital generated 15.3 times its net value in annual revenues. By itself, this is not especially revealing. But as part of a longer-term trend, as the turnover declines or grows, you gain some idea of how effectively management plans and controls its funds.

▨ Accounts Receivable Tests

The current asset account "accounts receivable" represents the balance of money owed to the company by its customers. Since some portion of receivables will eventually be written off as bad debts, the asset is reduced by a *reserve* for bad debts. Periodic entries are made into this reserve, offset by an annual bad debt expense. When accounts receivable are identified as bad debts, they are removed from the asset and from the reserve. The net asset consists of the asset account, minus the bad debt reserve. For example, accounts receivable are current $423,660 and the bad debt reserve is $7,215:

Accounts receivable	423,660
Reserve for bad debts	(7,215)
Net accounts receivable	416,445

The entry to increase bad debt reserve involves a credit to the reserve, offset by a debt to the expense account. For example, this year a company determines that its bad debt reserve should be increased by $900:

	Debit	Credit
Bad debt expense	900.00	
Reserve for bad debts		900.00

In the following year, if you decided that $450 is bad debt, it would look like this:

	Debit	Credit
Reserve for bad debts	450.00	
Accounts receivable		450.00

How much to place into the reserve is an accounting issue. Generally, a company will base its reserve decisions on its recent history of bad debts and current and anticipated changes in activity. The reserve is only an estimate, so actual levels are constantly adjusted.

The corporate policy regarding its reserve requirements can be tested with the *bad debts to accounts receivable ratio*. This formula, expressed as a percentage, should remain fairly level even when receivable levels grow. So if a company's revenues expand rapidly (meaning accounts receivable balances are likely to grow as well), you would not expect to see an increased percentage of bad debt reserves. No matter what dollar value of accounts receivable is on the books, the bad debt reserve should remain approximately the same on a percentage basis. The formula:

FORMULA: BAD DEBTS TO ACCOUNTS RECEIVABLE RATIO

$$\frac{B}{A} = R$$

> *where B = bad debts reserve*
> *A = accounts receivable*
> *R = bad debts to accounts receivable ratio*

Another way to track this asset is by comparing receivable levels to credit-based sales. You expect to see a consistent relationship between the two accounts. In other words, if accounts receivable is increasing at a greater rate than credit sales, that can spell trouble for working capital. The *accounts receivable turnover* is a calculation of this relationship. The formula:

FORMULA: ACCOUNTS RECEIVABLE TURNOVER

$$\frac{S}{A} = T$$

> *where S = credit sales*
> *A = accounts receivable*
> *T = accounts receivable turnover*

This formula may change drastically when the mix of business changes. So a company that either acquires a new subsidiary or spins off an operating unit might experience a change in this ratio (and many others). As with all ratio analysis, you develop reliable trends only when the values you use are consistent and accurate.

Another important test of how well a company is managing its accounts receivable is the *average collection period*, which tests the time required to collect debts. During times when revenues are expanding rapidly, there is a tendency to relax collection efforts and internal controls. As a consequence, you often see rapid growth accompanied by lower net profits. The collection period ratio is:

FORMULA: AVERAGE COLLECTION PERIOD

$$\frac{R}{S \div 365} = D$$

where R = accounts receivable
S = annual credit sales
D = average collection period (days)

For example, if the historical collection period is 48 days, but this suddenly increases to 74 days, there is a problem in collection procedures. Even with growth, you expect a corporation to exercise its controls, which include diligent collection enforcement.

Inventory Tests

In addition to cash, marketable securities, and accounts receivable, current assets include inventory. This is the value of goods the company holds for sale. Inventory is most often valued at actual cost, but numerous inventory valuation methods are in use and may affect profits. This becomes an issue in those organizations depending on significant inventory levels, notably manufacturing concerns. In manufacturing, inventory may be subdivided into several subcategories, including raw material, work in progress, and finished goods. In retail organizations, inventory tends to be turned over rapidly, as it is stored in warehouses for fast turnaround to retail outlets.

While inventory levels have to be expected to vary by industry, they may also vary by season. For example, you would expect to see higher inventory levels in the retail sector in the high-volume holiday season, and relatively low inventory levels in the first quarter. Identifying sectors can be elusive as well. For example, both

Microsoft and IBM are classified in the information technology sector, but their typical inventory levels are quite different. This is due to the subsector difference. Microsoft primarily sells software, whereas IBM primarily sells hardware. As a result, IBM carries at least twice the inventory level of Microsoft. Differences in revenue levels also affect this comparison. In the fiscal years 2006 and 2005, the two corporations reported:[6]

| | Inventory (in $millions) | |
	2006	2005
Microsoft	$1,478	$ 491
IBM	2,841	3,316

The complexity and variation of inventory levels makes it important that an accurate *average* inventory level be used in tracking inventory trends. The average inventory is determined in one of several ways. If inventory levels remain fairly consistent throughout the year, the beginning and ending balances may be added together and divided by 2. If quarterly levels change significantly, add quarter-end values together and divide by 4. In cases where inventory levels are quite volatile, monthly totals may be used. However, whereas quarterly and annual inventory values are readily found on corporate Web sites and on SEC filings, monthly totals are not as accessible. In the majority of instances, quarterly or annual averages will be sufficient. To compute *average inventory*, apply this formula:

FORMULA: AVERAGE INVENTORY

$$\frac{I^a + I^b + \cdots + I^n}{n} = A$$

$$
\begin{aligned}
\textit{where } I \quad &= \textit{inventory value} \\
a, b &= \textit{period used in calculation} \\
n \quad &= \textit{total number of periods} \\
A \quad &= \textit{average inventory}
\end{aligned}
$$

[6] Microsoft and IBM annual reports.

This average is used in calculation of *inventory turnover*, which is an estimate of the number of times inventory is sold and replaced. In actual practice, the goods in inventory are not completely disposed of and replaced; this is only an average. The turnover reflects management's efficiency at keeping inventory at the best possible level. If inventory levels go too high, this ties up cash and adds to storage costs and insurance. If levels go too low, it becomes increasingly difficult to fulfill orders and revenue is lost. To calculate inventory turnover:

FORMULA: INVENTORY TURNOVER

$$\frac{C}{A} = T$$

> *where C = cost of goods sold (annual)*
> *A = average inventory*
> *T = turnover*

Some formulas involve the use of sales in calculating inventory turnover. This is an unreliable alternative. Sales (or revenues) are recorded on a marked-up basis, whereas inventory is reported at actual cost. Using the cost of goods sold is much more accurate. So if a company reports annual cost of goods sold of $4.72 billion and average inventory of $1.09 billion, turnover is:

$$\frac{\$4.72}{\$1.09} = \textbf{4.3 turns}$$

This reveals that turnover occurred 4.3 times during the year. If the average has been in the range of 4.0 to 4.5, this is a typical year. However, if the turnover begins to decline in future years, that may be a sign that the company is investing too much in its inventory and better inventory controls are required.

Long-Term Asset Tests

While current assets define working capital trends, long-term assets (capital assets) may define the company's long-term commitment to growth and to creation of its own infrastructure.

By definition, a capital asset is any asset with a "useful life" greater than one to two years. When an asset is capitalized, it is set up as an asset (rather than as an expense) and written off over several years. The write-off is made in the form of annual depreciation.

VALUABLE RESOURCE:

To get information on depreciation rules and calculations, go to the Web site of the Internal Revenue Service, at www.irs.ustreas.gov and order form 4562 (depreciation instructions).

The IRS publishes charts with precalculated depreciation in many recovery classes. This includes depreciation for vehicles, machinery and equipment, and real estate. The basic formulas for calculating the best-known and most often used forms of depreciation are summarized below.

The easiest calculation is for *straight-line depreciation*, in which the same amount is deducted each year. The asset is divided by the number of years in the recovery period, and the result is the dollar amount of straight-line depreciation deducted each year. The formula:

FORMULA: STRAIGHT-LINE DEPRECIATION

$$\frac{A}{R} = D$$

where A = *basis of asset*
R = *recovery period*
D = *annual depreciation*

For example, a company purchases an asset worth $189,000. Its recovery period is seven years. Straight-line depreciation is:

$$\frac{\$189,000}{7} = \$27,000$$

A variation on this is declining-balance depreciation, which is calculated using either 150% or 200% of the straight-line method. For example, under the 200% method (200DB), the first year's depreciation is doubled; the basis for depreciation in the following year is the original basis minus the depreciation previously written off. The formula for *declining-balance depreciation* is:

FORMULA: DECLINING-BALANCE DEPRECIATION

$$\left(\frac{B - P}{R}\right) \times A = D$$

> where **B** = *basis of asset*
> **P** = *prior depreciation deducted*
> **R** = *recovery period*
> **A** = *acceleration percentage*
> **D** = *annual depreciation*

For example, a company purchases an asset for $189,000 and its recovery period is seven years. The annual depreciation for the first year using 200DB is:

$$\frac{\$189,000 - \$0}{7} \times 200\% = \$54,000$$

For the second year:

$$\frac{\$189,000 - \$54,000}{7} \times 200\% = \$38,571$$

The rules for deducting depreciation in the first year reduce the claimed amount, based on when the asset was purchased during the year. The same calculations using 150DB would be:

year 1: (($189,000 − $ 0) ÷ 7) × 150% = $40,500
year 2: (($189,000 − $40,500) ÷ 7) × 150% = $31,821

Capitalization

A lot of confusion arises about the concept of "capitalization," which often is confused with the vastly different "capital." A company's capital (or capital stock) is the value of shares sold to investors and outstanding. But capitalization includes capital as well as long-term debt. A company funds its operation through a combination of two sources: equity (capital) and debt (bonds and notes).

This is important because the makeup of capitalization varies considerably among companies within a single sector and between stocks that otherwise might look the same. You previously saw how the debt ratio (the percentage of debt to total capitalization) can and does vary widely. A high debt ratio demands a higher level of interest payments. In analysis of a company's balance sheet, the trend in the debt ratio is equally important. When you see a debt ratio emerge over a period of years in a very negative manner, it should provide you with a serious warning. For example, the trend shown for GM, Ford, and Lucent earlier in this chapter makes the point: When debt increases over time as a percentage of total capitalization, it is a highly negative indicator for equity investors.

A related indicator is the *dividend payout ratio* (also called *dividend cover*). This ratio compares dividends actually paid to earnings per share. As an investor, you hope to see a steady growth in both earnings and dividends over several years. This does not necessarily mean the dividend payout ratio has to increase each year, but as earnings grow, the percentage of dividend payout per share should remain the same. When you see this slipping over several years, it is a negative sign. The formula for dividend payout ratio is:

FORMULA: DIVIDEND PAYOUT RATIO

$$\frac{D}{E} = R$$

where D = dividend per share
E = earnings per share
R = dividend payout ratio

Both sides of the formula should be based on annual totals. And the same result is also found dividing actual dollar amounts of dividends and earnings. The per-share formula is more easily available and provides the more popular method for computation.

The dividend payout ratio provides you with a snapshot of a company's growth (positive or negative) over time. It is particularly revealing to compare payout ratio with debt ratio side by side. The most negative trend is in effect when you see debt ratio rising while dividend payout ratio declines each year.

A summary of dividend payout ratio for two tobacco companies reveals different trends in each:

	Dividend Payout Ratio	
Year	Altria	Reynolds American
2005	60%	63%
2004	62	34
2003	58	—
2002	47	80
2001	57	74

The interesting thing to observe in this side-by-side summary of the payout ratio is how the two companies differ. Altria's ratio has been fairly consistent, while Reynolds American's has been quite erratic. During the same period, Altria's debt ratio declined from 35% in 2001 to 24% at the end of 2005. Reynolds American's grew, but not by much. It went from 14% up to 18%.

Another comparison worth making is between two drug companies:

	Dividend Payout Ratio	
Year	Merck	Abbott Labs
2005	72%	50%
2004	57	51
2003	50	55
2002	45	51
2001	44	83

Important differences can be observed here as well. Merck's dividend payout ratio has been steady and, in 2005, jumped far ahead of the trend. Abbott Labs, in comparison, has a much smaller percentage payout over the same period. During this five-year period, Merck's debt ratio changed very little, remaining at or near 20% the entire time. Abbott Labs' debt ratio declined from 32% down to 23%, a very positive indicator.

The dividend payout ratio is an important test, not only of capitalization and cash flow, but also of very real growth. Even when a company's earnings per share grows over many years, if the dividend payout ratio slips and fails to keep pace, that is a very negative indicator. It is revealing to make comparisons within a market sector in order to make sound judgments about companies.

A final capitalization ratio worth checking is market capitalization, which is the overall value of stock on the market. It summarizes the actual market value based on what investors are willing to pay for stock. It has nothing to do with market value per share. For example, a company with one million shares selling for $40 per share is worth exactly the same as another company with two million shares selling for $20 per share. So you cannot rely on the share price to compare one company to another. When you perform side-by-side comparisons of companies, you need to look at *market capitalization* to make a valid analysis. The formula:

FORMULA: MARKET CAPITALIZATION

$$S \times P = C$$

> *where S = shares issued and outstanding*
> *P = price per share*
> *C = market capitalization*

The distinctions in the market regarding market capitalization are important because they define risk levels, price volatility, and investment desirability. Some investors diversify their portfolios based on market capitalization, for example. The largest corporations (mega cap) report market capitalization of $200 billion or more; while the exact size of different levels is not precise, large cap generally covers a range between $10 to $200 billion; mid cap

$2 to $10 billion; and small cap any company with market capitalization under $2 billion.

The study of capitalization and "size" of the company is easily misunderstood. Many investors make quick decisions based on stock price alone, believing that an $80 stock is more valuable than a $70 stock, without regard to market capitalization. A test worth making to further quantify the value of a company is the *common stock ratio*, or the percentage of total capitalization represented by common stock. This is the offset of the debt ratio if there is no preferred stock or other components to total capitalization. You can track the stock value of a company over time, which essentially reflects not only the book value of common equity, but also the market success of the stock. If a company's stock has risen in value over time, its common stock ratio will rise as well. The formula:

FORMULA: COMMON STOCK RATIO

$$\frac{S}{C} = R$$

> where S = *common stock issued and outstanding*
> C = *total capitalization*
> R = *common stock ratio*

The comparison between common stock and debt will be revealing over a period of years. When the common stock ratio declines over time, it is just as negative as seeing the debt ratio climb. When you see a consistent record over time, that indicates capital strength. For example, Wal-Mart's common stock ratio has remained between 63% and 67% for the five fiscal years of 2002 through 2006, a period of great market change and price volatility, especially in the retail sector. The consistency of the ratio is reassuring to investors.

Tangible and Total Book Value

A final area worth testing—and often overlooked entirely—is the test of actual book value of a company. Three tests are important.

First is the basic *book value per share*. This is a calculation of the per-share value of what the company reports. The net worth of a company is supposed to represent real value, although important adjustments often need to be made. The formula for book value per share is:

FORMULA: BOOK VALUE PER SHARE

$$\frac{N - P}{S} = B$$

> *where N = net worth*
> *P = preferred stock*
> *S = average shares issued and outstanding*
> *B = book value per share*

The preferred stock value is removed from total equity because the usual calculation of book value is understood on a "per common share" basis. When preferred stock value is substantial, it would distort the calculation. Calculating "average" shares outstanding requires an averaging between the beginning and end of the year and weighting that average to reflect a true average. For example, if a new issue occurred near the beginning of the fiscal year, it would have to be weighted to reflect a true overall average for the entire year.

A variation on this formula is *tangible book value per share*, which is isolated to only the tangible assets. Many corporations assign substantial value to goodwill and other intangible assets, distorting the value of the company's real book value. In comparing one company to another, variations in the value of intangible assets will make comparisons invalid. For this reason, tangible book value is more popularly used. The formula:

FORMULA: TANGIBLE BOOK VALUE PER SHARE

$$\frac{N - P - I}{S} = B$$

> *where N = net worth*
> *P = preferred stock*

I = *intangible assets*
S = *average shares issued and outstanding*
B = *tangible book value per share*

This formula includes one additional adjustment to the previous one, which is the removal of intangible assets from the net worth side of the equation. While book value often has little to do with the current market value of the stock, it is an important element worth tracking. For example, GM reported $18.12 tangible book value per share at the end of 2005, but a year earlier it had been $40.35. Shareholders suffered a decline of over half the company's book value in a single year.

Finally, the *core tangible book value per share* tells the real story. But information is not easy to find because core net worth is not reported in research reports or in company annual reports. The formula:

FORMULA: CORE TANGIBLE BOOK VALUE PER SHARE

$$\frac{N - P - I + (-)\,C}{S} = B$$

where N = net worth
P = preferred stock
I = intangible assets
C = core net worth adjustments
S = average shares issued and outstanding
B = core tangible book value per share

The only way to calculate this is based on news stories concerning unlisted liabilities. For example, it has been widely reported that as of 2005, GM owed $37 billion in pension liabilities. Its own annual report footnoted this amount, but it does not show up as a liability. Based on what is shown by GM, core tangible net worth would be negative if the $37 billion is assumed to have remained unchanged between 2004 and 2005:

	General Motors, Net Worth (in $millions)		
Year	Reported	Adjustment	Core Net Worth
2004	$14,597	$ − 37,000	$ − 22,403
2005	27,726	− 37,000	− 9,274

Based on this simplified analysis of reported versus core tangible earnings, GM has a negative core earnings per share. This is an extreme case, but it points out the glaring flaws in the accepted reporting standards and rules. The reality of a situation, as reflected by the core tangible net worth, is that a company may have a *negative* value, but the accounting rules allow it to report positive value.

There are many valuable tests you can perform based on the balance sheet, and these have been summarized in this chapter. The next chapter looks at the most valuable ratios to perform on the operating statement. This is where you judge and compare revenues and earnings.

CHAPTER 7

FUNDAMENTALS

OPERATING STATEMENT TESTS YOU NEED TO KNOW

THE PREVIOUS CHAPTER EXPLAINED ANALYSIS OF BALANCE SHEET AC-COUNTS. That statement reports on the balances of asset, liability, and capital accounts as of a fixed date, usually the end of a quarter or year. The operating statement is a summary of a series of transactions over a period of time, ending on a specific date. The period covered by the operating statement normally ends on the same date on which the balance sheet is prepared.

These two statements represent what most people are familiar with in terms of financial reporting. The balance sheet (ending date balances) and the operating statement (summary of transactions for a period of time) are supposed to reveal to you all that you need to know in order to make an informed opinion and to develop comparative value judgments about companies. For this, funda-mental analysis is based on a series of ratios and formulas intended to produce a shorthand version of the transactions (by way of per-centages, ratio index values, and numbers of turns). These repre-sentations are best reviewed under the following guidelines:

1. *Every ratio you use is best viewed as part of a long-term trend.* The ratio by itself can be compared to a universally accepted

standard, compared to your own goals, or looked at as the latest entry in a long-term trend. The longer the trend, the easier it is to understand the significance of the ratio. Even a two-year comparison has limited value compared to a five-year or a ten-year historical record.

2. *You need to take steps to ensure that comparisons are valid and accurate.* The problem with the fundamentals is their very complexity and variation. Validity is not as easily found as every investor would like. If one company has significant core earnings adjustments and another does not, it makes little sense to compare the reported numbers without adjusting them to the same basis (core earnings).

3. *Your ratios and formulas should reveal meaningful facts about risk and potential.* Any number of ratios can be used, but you should be sure you know how to interpret the results. What does a ratio reveal about the company? How can you equate a specific ratio in terms of income potential and risk? These are the key questions to ask about every ratio and every trend.

4. *Your program of fundamental analysis should employ a range of ratios and never a single indicator by itself.* Analysis becomes valuable when you review an entire series of trends, each developed from ratio tests. This does not mean you need to get an accounting education. In fact, using a handful of well-selected ratios is easy, and much of the work may be done for you already. Using a well-structured analytical service like the S&P Stock Reports provides a 10-year summary and includes most of the ratios you are likely to want in your program.

5. *Remember, a set of conclusions for one industry may not be comparable to the same conclusions in another industry.* One of the most common errors is to develop a series of assumptions about what outcomes should be, and then apply those assumptions to all companies. The truth is that every sector and subsector involves companies in particular industry groups, and these are, by definition, different from the companies in other sectors. Once you have decided which set of ratios to use, it makes sense to go through a review of an entire industry, de-

velop a working idea of the standards, and adjust your expectations based on those standards. Even the most basic ratios, such as the percentage of earnings, gross profit, expense levels, and other well-known tests, are going to be different between industries.

6. *The value judgments you develop should be employed as part of a specific goal.* When you begin to invest, you need to set goals for yourself. Most people understand this in terms of price appreciation, and they set goals based on that: "If the stock doubles in value, I will sell" or "If I lose 25%, I will cut my losses" are common price-based goal statements. The same strategic approach works with the fundamentals as well, and may be based on the ratios themselves, involving tests of working capital, capitalization ratios, revenue and earnings growth, or—in the best approach of all—a combination of all these critical areas of analysis.

The Basics of the Operating Statement

The operating statement summarizes revenues, costs and expenses, and earnings for a specified period of time. That time is usually a fiscal quarter or year, and the report normally includes the current period and the previous period so that comparisons are readily made. In corporate financial statements, the major expenses are summarized in a single line, so detailed analysis requires further investigation (this often means contacting the company's shareholder relations department and requesting breakdowns beyond what is shown on the published financial statement).

The components of the operating statement are summarized in Figure 7.1.

Because there are so many divisions to the operating statement, it is imperative to understand which line is being discussed and compared. "Earnings" should mean the same thing when comparing one company to another. The operating profit is normally used to report earnings per share, but important distinctions have to be made between the various kinds of *margins* found on the operating

FIGURE 7.1. OPERATING STATEMENT.

Company Name
Operating Statement

For the period January 1, 20xx
through December 31, 20xx

Revenues	xxx
Less: Cost of Goods Sold	–xxx
Gross Profit	xxx
Less: Expenses	–xxx
Operating Profit	xxx
Plus (minus) Other Income and Expenses	xxx
Pretax Profit	xxx
Less: Provision for Income Taxes	–xxx
After-Tax Profit	xxx

statement. These distinctions are shown later in this chapter. Below is a brief summary of operating statement divisions and terms:

Revenue. The top line is revenue (sales), and it is perhaps the best-known line and most often watched indicator on the operating statement. As a general observation, many people believe that as long as revenues are rising each year, all is well. But in reality, you are also likely to see rising revenue accompanied by falling earnings (net profits). That indicates that growth in terms of rising revenues is not always a positive attribute; it is always better when revenues *and* earnings both rise.

Cost of goods sold. This segment of the operating statement is the sum of several accounts. These include merchandise purchased for sale (or manufacture), freight, direct labor (salaries and wages paid to employees directly generating revenues), and a change in inventory levels from the beginning to the end of the period. A distinction is made between costs and expenses. Costs are expected to track revenues closely, and the percentage of costs should remain about the same even when revenue levels change. In comparison, expenses are assumed to be unresponsive to revenues. In situations where companies expand into new markets or product areas merge with other companies, expense levels will naturally change as well. But expenses can and should be controlled so that ever-greater profits can be achieved in periods of revenue growth.

Gross profit. This subtotal is the dollar amount of revenues minus costs. The percentage of gross profit is called gross margin. Just as direct costs should track sales closely, the gross profit should do the same. When you see a widely fluctuating gross margin from one period to the next, further analysis is required. Possible reasons include seasonal change, merger or acquisition, development of a new product line, sale of an operating unit, changes in inventory valuation method, or lack of internal controls.

Expenses. This category is the most varied and complex. It includes all money going out of the company as well as debts owed at the end of the period that are not *direct* in relation to revenue production. The distinction between direct costs and expenses is quite important in financial statement analysis because you expect, as a general rule, to see actual internal controls having the greatest impact in this portion of the operating statement. This relationship is demonstrated in Figure 7.2. Note how the changes occur as revenue and costs increase or decrease. First, revenue and costs track on the same trend, as you would expect. Skip to the bottom and you see the area of

FIGURE 7.2. OPERATING STATEMENT RELATIONSHIPS—WITH CONTROLLED EXPENSES.

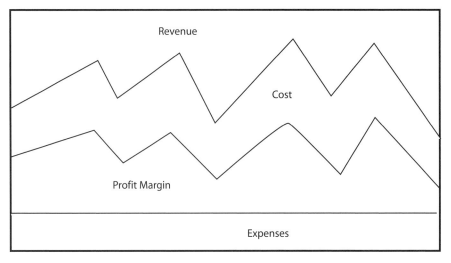

expenses, which is flat as you would expect. If this trend continues, the profit margin grows when revenues grow, and shrinks when revenues shrink.

Now consider what happens when expenses are not controlled. In that situation, the level of expenses tends to rise over time and does not retreat if and when revenues decline. As a consequence, the profit margin shrinks even when revenues rise and shrinks severely when revenues fall. This relationship is summarized in Figure 7.3. Note how much difference gradually increasing expenses makes. Expenses rise regardless of revenue and cost trends. At the end of the chart, revenues decline so that the profit margin shrinks considerably. Finally, it ends up in the territory of net losses. When a company experiences a net loss, it is usually due to a combination of events, including reduced revenues, nonrecurring adjustments or noncore losses, and—most severe of all—uncontrolled expenses.

The level of expenses can also be further subdivided, although the published annual reports and financial statements do not always provide these details. For example, two major subdivisions are selling expenses (those expenses related to

FIGURE 7.3. OPERATING STATEMENT RELATIONSHIPS—WITH UNCONTROLLED EXPENSES.

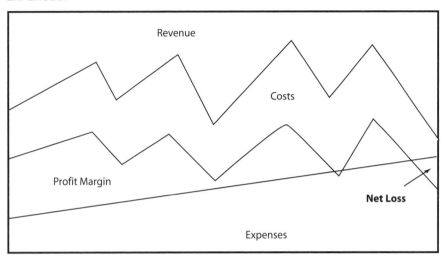

generation of sales, but not as directly as direct costs) and general and administrative expenses, also called overhead. These expenses recur each year regardless of revenue levels, and include administrative salaries and wages, rent, office telephone, and office supplies, for example.

Operating profit. This is the profit from operations, which, in most instances, will be the same as (or close to) S&P-defined core earnings. If the company has done a good job of isolating nonoperating expenses below this line, then this is a reliable number, but companies do not always make these matters clear. In fact, they may be obscured by an application of inconsistent standards, even with the blessing of the GAAP system. Another problem arises from the fact that published earnings per share are usually computed on the bottom line (after-tax profit), which is likely to include an array of nonoperational items. To gauge the significance of this distortion, compare the EPS on a reported basis with the EPS on a core earnings basis. For example, compare reported EPS and CEPS for three corporations over five years:[1]

[1] Annual statements and Standard & Poor's Stock Reports.

Earnings per Share

Year	Lucent Reported	Lucent Core	IBM Reported	IBM Core	Motorola Reported	Motorola Core
2005	$ 0.24	$ 0.06	$4.91	$3.93	$ 1.82	$ 1.18
2004	0.42	0.19	4.94	4.06	0.90	0.78
2003	−0.29	0.50	4.34	3.00	0.38	0.08
2002	−3.51	−4.86	3.07	0.08	−1.09	−0.93
2001	−4.18	−3.87	4.35	1.33	−1.78	−2.23

These comparisons between reported EPS and CEPS demonstrate that the changes are all over the board. So while operating profit is assumed to be the most reliable core earnings number (assuming it is truly an operating profit not affected by core earnings adjustments), the actual EPS reported by corporations and used by analysts is highly unreliable in many instances.

Other income and expenses. Following the operating profit are a series of additional adjustments, all part of the noncore or nonoperational section. In an ideal world, *all* core earnings adjustments would show up here, so that the operating profit could be a universally understood, consistent number. But because so many core earnings adjustments involve expenses not listed on the operating statement, this is not likely to occur any time in the near future. Other income includes profits from the sale of capital assets, currency exchange adjustments, interest income, and the sale of operating units. Other expenses includes losses from the sale of capital assets, currency exchange losses, interest expenses, and other noncore forms of income.

Pretax profit. When you add or subtract the net difference between other income and other expenses from operating profit, you find the pretax net profit. This is the value often used in analysis to report net earnings, but because it includes the effect of other income and expenses, this is less than accurate; and when comparing return on sales among different companies, there will be a lot of variation in the pretax profit.

Provision for income taxes. Companies set up reserves to pay income taxes, and this provision appears here as the second-to-last line of the operating statement. This value can change considerably and for a number of reasons. First, a company may be reducing its tax liability with carryover losses. Second, tax reporting is not always the same as GAAP reporting, so differences in the taxable net income or loss will affect the provision. Third, companies operating in foreign countries may pay a higher or lower overall tax rate depending on their mix of profits. Fourth, companies based in states that do not tax corporate profits will pay lower taxes than those in states with state-level income tax laws on the books.

After-tax profit. This is the "net net" profit or loss, the bottom line most often used to calculate EPS. The problem with this is that, as the previous explanations demonstrated, the after-tax profit is subject to many accounting interpretations, nonrecurring and noncore adjustments, and other factors, making a true comparison between companies less than reliable. Only the operating profit provides an approximation of outcome that can be treated as comparable, but EPS is usually reported on the basis of the bottom line, so investors get a distorted view of a company and its value and profitability.

Revenue Trends

Beginning at the top line of the operating statement, analysis begins by tracking revenue trends. Just about every analyst wants to see revenues grow each year. However, each sector involves competing companies and finite markets, so it is not realistic to expect every well-managed company to increase its revenue every year without fail.

Even when corporate revenues do grow, investors and analysts may have unrealistic expectations about the rate of growth. In other words, if a company increased revenues by 5% the first year, 10% percent the second year, and 15% the last year, should you expect a 20% growth rate this year? All statistics tend to level off over time, but that does not mean a slowdown in the rate of growth is bad news; it is simply reality.

The most popular method for tracking revenue is by year-to-year percentage change (up or down) in revenues. This is a reasonable method for tracking revenues because it ignores the dollar amount and reduces growth to a simple percentage. If a company's annual growth *rate* remains consistent or shows little change, that is far more positive in the long term than the less realistic demand for ever-higher rates of growth. To calculate the *rate of growth in revenue*, the formula is:

FORMULA: RATE OF GROWTH IN REVENUE

$$\frac{C - P}{P} = R$$

> *where C = current year revenue*
> *P = past year revenue*
> *R = rate of growth in revenue*

It is more revealing to compare *rate* of growth (plus or minus) than to review the dollar values of revenue from year to year. To demonstrate this, consider the case of three companies in the information technology sector (communications equipment subsector). First, the dollar value of revenue over a five-year period:[2]

	Revenue (in $millions)		
Year	Lucent Technologies	Avaya	Harris Corp.
2005	$9,441	$4,902	$3,001
2004	9,045	4,069	2,519
2003	8,470	4,338	2,093
2002	12,321	4,956	1,876
2001	21,294	6,793	1,955

At first glace, it appears that Lucent, as the largest volume producer among these competing companies, may be the best capitalized and offer the greatest growth potential. But in any revenue analysis, you also need to closely review profitability, and, as you will see later in this chapter, Lucent's high revenue volume is not sufficient to draw any conclusions. In terms of overall growth in revenue, the analysis

[2] Lucent Technologies, Avaya, and Harris Corporation annual reports.

takes on a clearer significance when reviewed in terms of year-to-year change:

| | Change in Revenue | | |
Year	Lucent Technologies	Avaya	Harris Corp.
2005	4.4%	20.5%	19.1%
2004	6.8	−6.2	20.4
2003	−31.3	−12.5	11.6
2002	−42.1	−27.0	−4.0
2001	−37.0	−11.5	8.2

An analyst looking at the dollar values of revenue might conclude that both Avaya and Harris are relatively small companies compared to Lucent, and not worthy candidates for long-term growth. If you were to base your analysis solely on revenue trends, it is possible to isolate only bigger-volume corporations in this manner. However, both Lucent and Avaya reported rates of revenue growth in negative double digits for three of the five years. Only Harris, the smallest of the three companies in this comparison, showed positive results, with plus-side double digit growth in three of the five years. While this conclusion is possible with a review of dollar values, it is more readily apparent when you review the rates rather than the dollars.

Earnings Trends

The trends in actual growth should not be restricted to revenue but should include earnings as well. Only in this way can you understand the importance of revenue growth. If a company reports increases in revenue but losses in the same years, that is far from a positive outcome.

The study of earnings can be done on a percentage basis just as revenues can be, and you will gain greater insight into the trend by performing an analysis on this basis. Using net profits to conform to the common practice among analysts is not acceptable, because of the potential for large core earnings adjustments. Accordingly, there are two formulas involved in the analysis of earnings. The traditional *rate of growth in earnings* is calculated with this formula:

$$\frac{C - P}{P} = E$$

> where C = *current year net earnings*
> P = *past year net earnings*
> E = *rate of growth in net earnings*

Using the same companies as used in the revenue example, the dollar value of traditional earnings was:

Year	Net Earnings (in $millions)		
	Lucent Technologies	Avaya	Harris Corp.
2005	$ 1,185	$ 923	$202
2004	2,002	291	126
2003	− 770	− 88	60
2002	− 11,826	− 666	83
2001	− 14,170	− 352	21

When the same results are expressed by rate of change, the picture becomes clearer:

Year	Change in Net Earnings		
	Lucent Technologies	Avaya	Harris Corp.
2005	− 40.8%	217.2%	60.3%
2004	360.0	355.7	110.0
2003	93.5	86.8	27.7
2002	20.4	− 47.1	295.2
2001	− 943.0	6.1	− 16.0

A more accurate rendition of earnings requires analysis of core earnings rather than reported net earnings. The formula for *rate of growth in core earnings* is:

FORMULA: RATE OF GROWTH IN CORE EARNINGS

$$\frac{CC - PC}{PC} = E$$

where CC = *current year core earnings*
PC = *past year core earnings*
E = *rate of growth in core earnings*

For these companies, the dollar-value outcomes were:

	Core Earnings (in $millions)		
Year	Lucent Technologies	Avaya	Harris Corp.
2005	$ 202	$ 876	$188
2004	754	252	120
2003	− 1,980	− 125	41
2002	− 16,627	− 997	37
2001	− 13,160	− 257	− 61

There are substantial differences between reported earnings and core earnings for Lucent; in fact, the overall adjustment for five years exceeded $7.2 billion. This means that under the GAAP method, profits were overstated (or, more precisely, losses were understated) by $7.2 billion. In comparison, the same adjustments for Avaya and Harris were negligible. On a rate of growth basis, the core outcomes were:

	Change in Core Earnings		
Year	Lucent Technologies	Avaya	Harris Corp.
2005	− 73.2%	247.6%	65.8%
2004	138.1	301.6	192.7
2003	880.9	87.5	10.8
2002	− 26.3	− 287.9	160.7
2001	NA	NA	NA

The 2001 changes were not available, since core earnings calculations date back only to 2001. Note in this comparison that only minor percentage changes applied to Avaya and Harris, whereas Lucent's core earnings changes were highly volatile. In addition, Harris—the smallest of the three—reported *positive* core earnings growth through the entire five-year period.

These types of analysis—using percentage changes and comparing revenues to core earnings—provide the most meaningful conclusions on top-line and bottom-line change over time. This is the most reliable operating statement trend analysis, especially when you understand the flaws in GAAP reporting and how those flaws distort the fundamental analysis itself.

▪ Revenue Compared to Direct Costs and Expenses

Within the operating statement, you will find additional valuable information for selecting companies. To better understand the causes of trends in revenue and earnings, begin with an analysis of the relationship between revenue and gross profit. If the gross profit is inconsistent from year to year, you can expect to see a corresponding inconsistency in reported profits or losses.

Direct costs—expenditures that are related specifically to generation of revenues—should remain constant from year to year. The costs—including merchandise as the primary element—will change in percentage terms only due to changes in valuation methods for inventory, catastrophic inventory losses, or changes in the mix of business. A change can be brought about through mergers or as a consequence of selling off an operating segment. But assuming that none of those unusual events occur, you should be able to track direct costs and gross profit and see consistency from year to year.

When you deduct direct costs from revenue, you find the gross profit. The percentage of gross profit to revenue is called *gross margin*. The formula for checking the gross margin is:

FORMULA: GROSS MARGIN

$$\frac{G}{R} = M$$

where G = gross profit

R = revenue

M = gross margin

For example, IBM reported revenues, direct costs, and gross profit for three years as:[3]

	In $millions		
	2005	*2004*	*2003*
Revenue	$91,134	$96,293	$89,131
Direct costs	54,602	60,724	56,584
Gross profit	$36,532	$35,569	$32,547
Gross margin	40.1%	36.9%	36.5%

The consistency of gross margin in this example makes the point that direct costs as a percentage of revenue should not vary greatly from year to year. So from 2003 to 2004, gross margin changed by only 0.4%; and from 2004 to 2005, it changed only 3.2%.

The analysis becomes even more revealing when expenses are studied in relation to revenue, and when changes in expenses are reviewed on a percentage basis. The formula for *rate of growth in expenses* is:

FORMULA: RATE OF GROWTH IN EXPENSES

$$\frac{C - P}{P} = E$$

where C = current year expenses

P = past year expenses

E = rate of growth in expenses

IBM's summary showed the following for expenses:

	In $millions		
	2005	*2004*	*2003*
Expenses	$27,156	$25,953	$23,915
Rate of growth	5.0%	8.5%	

[3] IBM annual reports.

While a short-term analysis such as this provides only limited information, it allows you to view the trend and to better understand how the top and bottom lines have evolved. To a degree, changes in expense levels are also going to be a factor of changes in revenue. While expense levels are not directly related to revenue, they have to be expected to change to some degree as revenue moves. In the example, IBM's revenue grew more than $7 billion from 2003 to 2004, and then fell more than $5 billion in 2005. Some effect has to be expected in expense levels. For this reason, expenses also need to be reviewed through the formula for *ratio of expenses to revenue*, which is:

FORMULA: RATIO OF EXPENSES TO REVENUE

$$\frac{E}{R} = P$$

> *where E = expenses*
> *R = revenue*
> *P = ratio (percentage)*

In the case of IBM, this ratio for the three years shown was:

	In $millions		
	2005	*2004*	*2003*
Revenue	$91,134	$96,293	$89,131
Expenses	27,156	25,953	23,915
Ratio	29.8%	27.0%	26.8%

The change from year to year is insignificant in this case, indicating that internal controls are being well enforced. Recalling the volatility in revenue levels for the three years, the consistency in the expense ratio is a very positive sign.

A final level of analysis is based on the operating profit. The previous formulas show how the items between the top and bottom lines are studied, and how they affect the overall results. The operating profit—assumed to be the profit from all core activities or, as most companies refer to it, from continuing operations—is the number to watch when trying to quantify growth potential. The first of two formulas to study is the *rate of growth in operating profit*, which is not the same as the previously introduced rate of growth in net earnings. That formula includes all other income and expenses and is normally based on the after-tax profit. Operating profit is limited to earnings from operations and is computed by the following formula:

FORMULA: RATE OF GROWTH IN OPERATING PROFIT

$$\frac{C - P}{P} = R$$

> where C = *current year operating profit*
> P = *past year operating profit*
> R = *rate of growth in operating profit*

IBM's operating profit is computed by subtracting expenses from gross profit. The company reported the following operating profit for three years:

	In $millions		
	2005	2004	2003
Operating profit	$9,376	$9,616	$8,632
Rate of growth	−2.5%	11.4%	

An additional formula is equally important for long-term trend watching. This is the *operating profit margin*, which is:

FORMULA: OPERATING PROFIT MARGIN

$$\frac{E}{R} = M$$

> where E = *expenses*
> R = *revenue*
> M = *operating profit margin*

For example, IBM reports its three-year outcome as:

	In $millions		
	2005	2004	2003
Revenue	$91,134	$96,293	$89,131
Direct costs	54,602	60,724	56,584
Gross profit	$36,532	$35,569	$32,547
Expenses	27,156	25,953	23,915
Operating profit	$9,376	$9,616	$8,632
Margin	10.3%	10.0%	9.7%

Even with the volatility in revenue, the company produced very consistent operating profits during these three years. It should be clear from an evaluation of these many versions of "income," "profits," and "earnings" that the many terms only confuse the issue. The accounting industry is a passive and reactive culture; it is not in its interests to improve the terminology used in financial reporting, although it should be. Ultimately, it will be up to corporate leaders to achieve true transparency.

As an investor, you ensure that your comparisons are truly valid by following these guidelines:

1. *Study the terminology to ensure that you're using comparable values.* Not every company uses the same phrasing for the various levels on the operating statement. One may refer to *net income*, another to *income from continuing operations*. But are these truly comparable? The value used affects not only return on sales, but also P/E ratio and EPS, among the important ratios popularly followed.

2. *Remove noncore income and add excluded expenses to reported earnings, to ensure accuracy.* The inclusion of noncore income and exclusion of core expenses is a significant problem in the accounting/auditing culture *and* in the corporate reporting culture as well. Unfortunately, the reporting formats considered official and correct are unreliable and misleading. You need to seek out the true core earnings from operations to develop reliable long-term trends.

3. *Pay close attention to the differences between reported and core earnings.* You will discover in reviewing the long-term trends for many companies that there is a close relationship between core earnings adjustments and volatility (both in revenues and in stock prices). As a general rule, companies with relatively high core earnings adjustments are also going to experience higher than average stock price volatility. And those with low core earnings adjustments will be far less volatile. Rather than simply accepting reported net earnings, use the core earnings value as the most reliable indicator of where earnings are leading into the future.

The relationship between the fundamentals and a stock's price volatility is direct. The two camps (fundamental and technical) complement one another, and should not be thought of as different or separate. The next chapter provides you with valuable technical formulas that can be used, along with fundamental tests, to evaluate risks and to pick stocks.

CHAPTER 8

TECHNICALS

PRICE AND VOLUME CALCULATIONS

THE FUNDAMENTALS INVOLVE FINANCIAL STATEMENTS, earnings reports, dividend declarations and payments, and other financially based information. As such, fundamental analysis involves looking backward to the historical facts in order to develop a sense of the trends and estimate where the future is heading. In comparison, technical analysis is based on today's price and volume facts and is focused on how trading trends affect price.

In using technical factors, it is wise to keep a few guidelines in mind:

1. *Technical and fundamental analysis can be used together for cross-confirmation.* The various indicators you track in a fundamental program often work well when augmented with specific technical indicators and ratios. Neither point of view has an exclusive on being right more than the other; all analysis involves estimates. The more valid information you employ, the better. Looking to historical information exclusively and ignoring current price trends is a mistake, and restricting your analysis to price without also checking profitability and capital strength is equally misguided.

2. *Technical trends are valuable for identifying risk levels.* Even when a company has adequate capitalization and a strong and consistent record of managing debt, creating higher revenue and earnings, and paying dividends, this does not tell the whole story. If you check price volatility, you discover that many companies that are equal in terms of fundamental strength often have far different volatility levels. This defines market risk and is a factor you cannot afford to ignore. Based on your individual risk profile, you might prefer low-volatility stocks, or be willing to accept greater volatility in order to also expose yourself to greater profit potential.

3. *Many technical trends signal changes in fundamental trends.* Many investors believe that the fundamentals and technicals operate distinctly and differently from each other. But you cannot ignore either side because they work interchangeably. A change in stock price volatility often foreshadows surprises in earnings reports, for example. The tendency is to think that earnings news creates reaction in price, which may be true, but the action-reaction cycle works in the other direction as well.

■ The Basics of Technical Analysis

Technical analysis is premised on one feature: the stock's price and trends in price movement. A related feature, volume, is also considered in interpreting stock price movement. A primary feature of technical analysis is the attempt to anticipate the next direction a stock's price is likely to move, and to invest either long or short accordingly; to time not only purchase decisions, but sale or hold decisions as well; and to improve the percentage of correct timing estimates based on techniques such as chart watching, price and volume formulas, and observation of price trading ranges.

The underlying premise of technical analysis is found in the Dow Theory. Although this theory is most often applied to market-wide indices like the Dow Jones Industrial Average (DJIA), its precepts can also be used to technically analyze individual stocks.

Charles Dow, cofounder of Dow Jones & Company, developed the initial theory in the 1880s and 1890s. Originally, Dow intended his theories to be applied to business models in predicting revenue and other financial trends. Dow was also interested in tracking his theories to predict market movements, and he developed the concept of using an index of typical stocks to track and develop trends. Dow himself did not develop what is today known as the Dow Theory. After his death in 1902, Samuel Nelson, an associate, published a book called *The ABCs of Stock Speculation*. In this book, Nelson referred to many of Charles Dow's essays as a premise for predicting market change.

The basic premise of the Dow Theory is that stock prices tend to act in concert; when the trend is upward, the overall market trends in that direction, and vice versa. So a limited number of market leaders can be identified and most other stocks will follow the lead established by those influential companies. This led to the identification of 30 stocks that today make up the best-known average, the DJIA. Taken together, these 30 companies represent about 25% of the total value of all companies listed on the New York Stock Exchange (NYSE).[1]

Under the Dow Theory, some very specific concepts mandate how trend analysis takes place. There are three recognized trends that technicians track. First is the daily trend, also called the market's tertiary movement, which is not reliable for the purposes of developing actual longer-term trends. Second is a 20-to-60-day trend, also called a secondary movement and reflecting current sentiment. Finally, a primary movement represents the overall long-term market sentiment and may last between several months and several years. The primary trend underway at any moment is usually described as a bull market (upward moving) or a bear market (downward moving).

In addition to distinguishing the types of trends from one another, the Dow Theory requires that any indicated change in a trend be confirmed. Under the beliefs of the Dow Theory, the Dow Jones Transportation Average has to change in the same way as the DJIA, in order to establish as fact that a change in direction has occurred. So if and when one of the two averages falls below previ-

---

[1] Dow Jones & Company Web site, http://djindexes.com/mdsidx/index.cfm?event=showAvgStats#cmc.

ous lows in successive declines, or above previously established highs in successive rallies, it does not signal a change in the primary trend until the second, confirming indicator follows suit.

These rules are important because they form the basic beliefs among technicians, or at least among those technicians who swear by the Dow Theory. Without a precise requirement in place to set a new direction, there would be no certainty as to whether a current trend had ended or merely paused. The DJIA serves an important function in the market by enabling investors to make judgments about the overall market at any time, based on the recent point changes, volume, and volatility of the market. But even the most faithful technicians should remember a few additional points:

1. *The index does not affect individual stocks.* The DJIA is a barometer of the entire market, but it should not be assumed to be an indicator of when to buy or sell individual stocks. Every stock changes in price due to numerous causes, including sector-wide trends, cyclical business changes, overall economic influences, activity among large institutional investors, competitive changes, and earnings reports. So any one of these or a combination of all of them will affect a stock's price from day to day, apart from what the index of 30 industrial stocks is doing at the same time.

2. *Every index is an average of several stocks, some advancing and some declining.* A strong point movement in the DJIA does not represent the entire market. In fact, every day's point change is the *net* difference between advancing and declining issues within the index. With this in mind, only market-wide composite indices can be expected to represent the real activity in the market. The DJIA is a valuable tool for gauging market sentiment but not for making decisions within a portfolio.

3. *The DJIA, like all indices, is a useful tool but not the final word.* All indicators add something to a body of knowledge about the market, whether in the moment or with a broader view. It is always a mistake to rely on any one indicator, however. The DJIA sets a tone and tells you what investment professionals, institutions, and other individuals are thinking. It summarizes

degrees of optimism or pessimism. But in evaluating how to act for your own portfolio, you need to use the DJIA as one of several useful indicators, and not as the last word.

The Random Walk Hypothesis and the Efficient Market Theory

The Dow Theory forms the basis for technical analysis of the stock market. There are additional theories about how and why prices change and what influences are at work in the market. The random walk hypothesis, for example, is a belief that all price change is arbitrary. This is based on the idea that current prices result from agreement among buyers and sellers in a complex understanding of stock share value. The random walk hypothesis is troubling to an army of well-paid insiders. If the hypothesis is correct, then those thousands of experts—analysts, managers, stockbrokers, and researchers—are of no real value. Cynically speaking, all price change is random.

If the random walk hypothesis is applicable, it also means that any stock you buy is going to be a 50-50 proposition. It will have an equal chance of rising or falling, according to the hypothesis. But like most theories, this one is flawed, and it can be demonstrably disproved. An analysis of long-term price trends reveals that well-managed companies produce profits, and that consistent growth in profits directly causes long-term increases in value. Many well-managed companies can be studied to make this point, just as poorly managed companies' stock falls on hard times. But it is not just poor management that causes these problems. For example, economic changes have affected the airline and auto industries. These same industries have competed over many years by creating attractive employee and retirement benefit programs, and these same programs have bankrupted many of the companies in those industries. Technology also affects corporate profitability and competitiveness. A few decades ago, Polaroid introduced the instant camera and revolutionized that industry; but with the emergence of the digital camera technology, the relatively expensive Land

Camera was no longer appealing, and Polaroid filed for bankruptcy.[2]

A similar trend can be seen even in large, well-capitalized corporations. Eastman Kodak has experienced several years of declining stock price levels *and* key fundamental indicators. In 1996, Kodak's stock ranged between $65 and $85 per share; in 2005, the range was between $21 and $35. The slide in prices reflects not only the problems of Kodak's continued dependence on old-style film products and a late entry into the digital camera market; it also reflects declining earnings along with increased debt levels:[3]

| | Earnings (in $millions) | | Debt |
Year	Reported	Core	Ratio
2005	$ − 1,455	$ − 1,419	58%
2004	81	− 119	33
2003	238	149	41
2002	793	127	30
2001	76	− 541	37

The volatility in earnings *and* the large disparities between reported and core earnings are danger signals that are also reflected in the deteriorating stock price over time. The point to this is that changes in key fundamental indicators (i.e., reported and core earnings and the debt ratio) are directly linked to stock prices and affect those prices over time. This challenges the random walk hypothesis directly. It would be difficult to find a company with declining fundamentals (revenue and earnings, debt ratio, etc.) that also experienced *rising* stock prices. It would be equally difficult to find a company with declining fundamentals whose stock price randomly changed from one year to another. The trend will invariably be to follow the bad news in the financial reports.

By the same argument, it would be unusual to see long-term good news in the financial statement accompanied by a declining stock price (or one moving randomly). In those cases where revenue and earnings rise consistently over time, when debt levels are

---

[2] Polaroid filed for Chapter 11 bankruptcy protection in 2001 after years of ever-higher long-term debt on its books. The company could not meet its nearly $1 billion in bond and note liabilities.
[3] Eastman Kodak annual reports.

kept low, and where other fundamental indicators remain strong, you also see rising stock values. These realities disprove the random walk hypothesis in the long term. However, most market theories, including the Dow Theory, discount the value of any short-term trends, so the random walk hypothesis may be applicable to price movement from one day to the next, regardless of long-term fundamental and technical trends.

A second market theory worth study is the efficient market theory. This theory simply states that the current prices of all stocks reflect all known information about a company. Bad news is already discounted in the price, and good news is already factored in. The efficient market theory is tidy and reassuring, but, like the random walk hypothesis, it is flawed. Short-term price movement is caused by an unknown variety of factors and tends to be overreactive to virtually all news and information. When a company's earnings are reported at $.02 per share lower than an analyst's estimates, the stock's price tumbles in overreaction, only to recover one or two days later. When a company's management announces that the coming year's earnings will be lower than the previous year's, the market overreacts yet again, even if the long-term fundamentals remain strong. For example, in November 2006, Wal-Mart announced that its October revenue levels were disappointing and a flat November was expected. The stock moved from $49.23 per share down to $47.24—a two-point drop—in two days, and then gradually recovered. The company has reported long-term growth in both revenue and earnings and is one of the market's success stories, but the short-term price overreacted to news about a single month's sales. This inefficiency is often witnessed in short-term pricing, even if the longer-term trend is more logical and efficient.

While the random walk hypothesis is more likely to apply in the short-term price trend, the efficient market theory is the opposite: It is more likely to apply in intermediate and long-term price trends, but not at all in the day-to-day price movement.

Basic Price Calculations

Because technical analysis focuses on price, it is also the most common form of information available today. To the extent that the stock market news is covered in the television and radio media, there are usually only three types of reports. First is specific company news, usually only local in nature (for example, if a major employer lands a new long-term contract, issues earnings reports, or lays off a large number of employees). Second is the daily change in the indices, especially the DJIA, which for most observers is "the market." Third and most popular is the day's change in a stock's price.

The changing stock price is almost always reported by the number of points. You will hear, for example, that a particular stock "lost two points in active trading" or that another stock rose "five points on positive earnings news." But what does this really mean? When you consider that the stock's price varies, a point change does not always mean the same thing. For example, what happens when two stocks both rise three points in a single day? One stock opened the day at $27 per share, and the other opened at $81:

Stock	Open	Close	Change	%
A	$27	$29	+2	7.4%
B	81	83	+2	2.5%

To compute the relevant *percentage price change*, the formula is:

FORMULA: PERCENTAGE PRICE CHANGE

$$\frac{C}{O} = P$$

where C = change
O = opening price
P = percentage price change

This is an important distinction. The percentage of change rather than points is what really counts. Consider the outcome when one stock opens at $27 and rises two points, and another stock opens at $81 and rises five points. On a percentage basis:

Stock	Open	Close	Change	%
A	$27	$29	+2	7.4%
B	81	86	+5	6.2%

If you had the same amount of money invested in both of these issues, the $27 stock would have outperformed the higher-priced $81 stock:

300 shares @ $27 =	$8,100	
2 points =	600	
increased value	$8,700	7.4%
100 shares @ $81 =	$8,100	
5 points =	500	
increased value	$8,600	6.2%

Because the lower-priced stock rose at a greater percentage, the increase in dollar value and percentage is greater as well. The difference in points—two versus five—is actually meaningless when you consider that the percentage change is more relevant.

Another way to look at price change is in the entire market. Rather than focusing on a single stock, the "mood of the market" can be judged based on several criteria. The most popular is through tracking one of several indices. The best-known are the DJIA, the S&P 500, and the NASDAQ Composite. The market can also be tracked by comparing stocks that have reached new high prices versus those reaching new low prices. The new levels are based on 52 weeks, and this ratio indicates whether the market trend is positive or negative. The more new highs, the more optimistic; and the more new lows, the more pessimistic.

The formula for *new high/new low ratio* is:

FORMULA: NEW HIGH/NEW LOW RATIO

$$\frac{H}{L} = R$$

where *H* = *number of issues with new high prices*
L = *number of issues with new low prices*
R = *new high/new low ratio*

Technical analysts also consider comparisons between advancing and declining issues to be important. In indices, the daily change represents the net difference when advances and declines are offset. But a test of the overall number of issues advancing and declining over the entire market provides a clearer view of the market's direction.

To compute the *advance/decline ratio*, the formula is:

FORMULA: ADVANCE/DECLINE RATIO

$$\frac{A}{D} = R$$

where A = *number of advancing issues*
D = *number of declining issues*
R = *advance/decline ratio*

Chart Patterns and Interpretations

Even when focusing on the formulas and ratios of technical analysis, you cannot avoid the price trends that show up in specific charting patterns. The whole premise of technical analysis is the study of price and price patterns. A limited number of classic technical patterns and concepts form the basis for a rudimentary appreciation of technical analysis.

The purpose in computing market mood and directions of trends is not only to time purchase and sale decisions but also to judge risk. Viewing price trends and patterns demonstrates the unavoidable risk/reward relationship. When price movement is highly volatile, opportunity is greater, but so is risk. Conservative investors prefer low-volatility stocks and in exchange accept the probability that prices will not move upward (or downward) rapidly.

The definition of volatility relies upon a basic technical tool, the trading range. Stocks tend to establish a limited number of points in which they trade. If and when price breaks through above or below this established range, it is a significant event, signaling a new rally or decline in the stock's price level. Technicians also observe that when price approaches the upper or lower limits on two or more consecutive attempts to break through, it often signals a price movement in the opposite direction.

The upper trading limit is also called *resistance level*. It is the highest price in the current trading range that buyers are willing to pay. The lower price limit is called *support level*, which is the lowest price that sellers are willing to accept upon sale of their stock. Once these well-defined lines are crossed, the trading range is likely to become more volatile, at least in the short term, until a new trading range has been set.

The trading range, resistance, and support are summarized in Figure 8.1.

Technicians are continually looking for revealing patterns in price trends. For example, a classic charting pattern is called head and shoulders, so named because it involves three high prices with the middle price (the head) being higher than the first and third price peaks (the shoulders). The head and shoulders pattern is seen as an attempt to break out above resistance. Upon retreat without successfully breaking through, the pattern indicates a pending price retreat. An inverse head and shoulders pattern (one in which low

FIGURE 8.1. TRADING RANGE, RESISTANCE, AND SUPPORT.

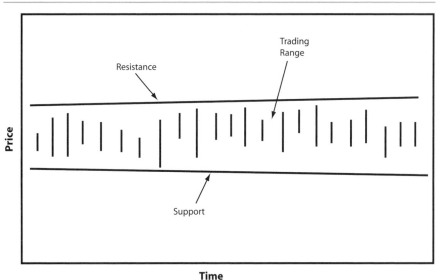

price levels are seen in place of high levels) indicates the opposite: After three unsuccessful attempts to move price below support level, the inverse head and shoulders is a signal that prices are about to move upward. Both of these patterns are summarized in Figure 8.2

When price moves above resistance or below support, it is called a *breakout*. A similar aberration in price patterns occurs through gaps. A *gap* occurs whenever the price closes on one day and opens above or below the trading range of the previous day (creating a visible price gap between the high and low range of each day).

The gap is important because it implies significant changes in trading range and interest among buyers (or the loss of interest among sellers). Four kinds of gaps are worth comparing: The common gap occurs as part of routine trading and does not signify big changes by itself. A breakaway gap moves price into new territory and does not retreat to fill in the gap in subsequent trading. A runaway gap is actually a series of gaps over several days, with price moving in the same direction. Finally, an exhaustion gap is likely to be quite large and signals the end of the runaway pattern, followed by price movement in the opposite direction.

The various types of gaps are summarized in Figure 8.3.

Many additional technical patterns are used by technicians, but these represent the major and most important signals. Tracking a stock's trading range reveals the degree of price volatility and, thus, market risk in a particular stock. The trading range—and its stability—is the best measure of this risk.

Technical Tests of Market Sentiment

Many additional technical indicators have been used by traders and analysts over many years to judge market sentiment and anticipate the direction of price movement. A word of caution: In the quickly changing market environment, many historical indicators may be less significant today than in the past. In addition, the actual meaning of some indicators could be different today due to widespread use of the Internet and improved information resources.

*FIGURE 8.2. HEAD AND SHOULDERS AND INVERSE HEAD AND SHOULDERS
PATTERNS.*

(a) head and shoulders

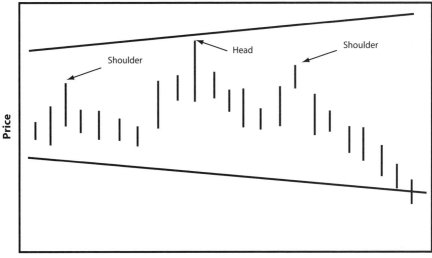

(b) inverse head and shoulders

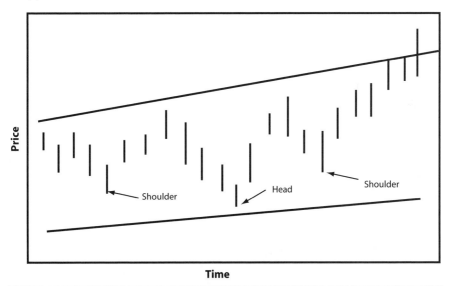

FIGURE 8.3. GAPS.

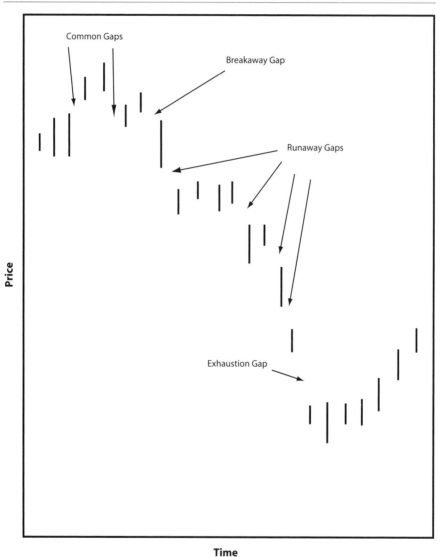

VALUABLE RESOURCE:

To find current market and trading statistics, check the New York Stock Exchange (NYSE) historical records site, at www.cftech.com/BrainBank/ FINANCE/NewYorkStockExch.html.

One of these traditional indicators is the *short interest ratio*. This is a contrarian indicator measuring the number of shares sold short. Most technicians who track short interest believe that as short sales increase, it is a sign that values are going to rise; and that when the numbers fall, it indicates that prices are going to fall. In other words, the contrarian viewpoint, that the majority is usually wrong, is the guiding theme behind this ratio. The formula:

FORMULA: SHORT INTEREST RATIO

$$\frac{S}{V} = R$$

where S = number of shares sold short
V = total trading volume
R = short interest ratio

One reason that short interest is difficult to track today is that short selling is not an investor's only bearish choice. In the past, an investor would sell short in the belief that share value was going to drop; then shares could be bought to close at a profit. But the short sale requires borrowing shares from the broker and then selling them, so there is an interest expense involved, not to mention significant risk. If share value rises, the short seller has to eventually close the position at a loss *and* pay interest. An alternative today is to buy put options. This achieves the same market position, one in which the trader profits if the stock's share price falls. But going long on puts is substantially less risky than selling stock short. It requires no payment of interest on borrowed shares. And potential losses are limited to the cost of the put.

With all of this in mind, short interest is a less definite measure of market sentiment and mood. Because of ever-growing involvement with options, improved access to the entire market, and rapid availability of information, the short interest ratio continues to provide an interesting insight to the market mood, but not as reliably as in the past.

Sentiment indicators are not as precise as many other formulas and ratios. A lot of time may be spent checking economic indicators and other trends outside of the immediate market issues. The question on everyone's mind is: What are price levels today, and what will they be tomorrow? To answer this question, sentiment indicators, economic trends, and other indirect influences on the market are less reliable than the tried and true technical signs: Emerging changes in trading range, price volatility, and volume.

Checking degrees of insider trading, tracking cyclical changes, and equating fundamental trends with technical reaction are all valid and useful indicators. But in the venue of technical analysis, focus is going to be more likely to remain on price and price trends.

Volatility

The trend in price volatility is a central issue to the technician. A trading range that remains within a few points is a sign of low volatility. So even as price levels evolve, the trading range may remain relatively narrow. In other words, price levels may be inching upward or downward over time, but the breadth of the trading range remains small. If and when a broadening formation emerges, that is a sign of coming change. Greater price volatility is best understood in terms of emerging changes in trading range.

A traditional method for measuring volatility involves comparisons of 52-week price levels. This formula for *volatility* is:

FORMULA: VOLATILITY

$$\frac{H - L}{L} = V$$

> *where H = 52-week high price*
> *L = 52-week low price*
> *V = volatility*

This is expressed as a percentage. For example, consider the 52-week price history for three stocks:

Stock A   22–28
Stock B   42–48
Stock C   62–68

Each of these stocks experienced a six-point spread through a 52-week period. But volatility is different for each based on the formula:

Stock A   (28 − 22) ÷ 22 = 27%
Stock B   (48 − 42) ÷ 42 = 14%
Stock C   (68 − 62) ÷ 62 = 10%

You might be inclined to think of a six-point trading range as low volatility, especially over an entire 52-week period. And that is true, but the traditional method of calculating volatility is flawed in one sense. All these stocks experienced a six-point trading range for the year. For this reason, a more reliable method for judging volatility could involve a rather simple comparison of the point spread itself. With this alternative method, all these stocks would have a volatility of "6"—six points over a 52-week period.

Another flaw in the traditional method of calculating volatility is that it does not allow for spikes in price. In most statistical analyses, a spike is considered out of the range, so it would be excluded. By definition, a spike in a stock's price occurs when the following conditions are met:

1. The price spike is substantially above or below the established trading range.

2. The price trading immediately returns to previously established levels.

3. The spike trading range is not repeated.

For example, consider the trading history of a stock trading between $22 and $28 per share for the entire year, with one exception. Based on a rumor that the company was about to be taken over by a competitor, the price jumped in a single day to $37 per share. The rumor proved to be unfounded, and the price retreated over the next two days to the established $22 to $28 range. Under the traditional measurement of volatility, the outcome would be:

(37 − 22) ÷ 22 = 68%

Removing the spike returns the volatility to a more realistic level:

(28 − 22) ÷ 22 = 27%

If you use the proposed point-based alternative, the 52-week range extends over 15 points, but the removal of the spike in price returns it to the more realistic level of 6 points.

The problem with the traditional method of calculating price volatility comes from two issues. First, the analysis is based on a percentage of variation, so that higher-priced stocks appear to have lower volatility (even when point spread, or trading-range breadth, is identical to that of lower-priced stocks). Second, the method ignores the ramifications of atypical price spikes outside of an es- tablished trading range. These may be caused by rumors, earnings surprises, and institutional investor activity, but as long as the spike is not permanent, it should be taken out of the equation.

If the traditional method is to be used, an *adjusted volatility* formula makes sense. The formula for this is:

FORMULA: ADJUSTED VOLATILITY

$$\frac{(H - L) - S}{L} = V$$

> *where H = 52-week high price*
> *L = 52-week low price*
> *S = price spikes*
> *V = adjusted volatility*

Application of this formula would be to adjust the 52-week range to a realistic range without spikes, and then employ the stan- dard volatility formula based on the adjusted levels. However, this method still provides only a percentage comparison, distorting the issue. A comparison at various price levels makes this point clearly. The higher the trading range, the lower the volatility.

Volume

Technicians study not only price, but trading volume as well. While price is easily comprehended, volume is not. You can see a price change and immediately grasp its implications. Stock value rises and it falls. But volume is a combination of activity by buyers and sellers. Exceptionally high volume may occur in a single day, but what does it mean?

A basic volume analysis may involve percentage-based *change in volume*, which tracks shares traded from day to day or from week to week. The formula:

FORMULA: CHANGE IN VOLUME

$$\frac{(C - P)}{P} = V$$

> *where C = current period volume*
> *P = past period volume*
> *V = change in volume*

This formula is useful in tracking change, especially if calculated using a moving average. Many Web sites providing charting service include price or volume moving average totals as part of the calculation. However, this does not tell you much about the underlying causes of volume changes. A more revealing formula is the *mutual funds cash/assets ratio*. This formula tracks not the volume itself, but the sentiment among institutional investors. Mutual funds and other institutions account for a majority of trading activity, while individuals ("retail" investors) are in the minority. So trading sentiment among mutual funds anticipates trading in the future; as the amount of total assets left in the form of cash increases, the indicators turn optimistic (because, as a contrarian indicator, the assumption is also built in that mutual fund management is usually wrong). This test is included as a test of volume trends specifically because it predicts those trends in a contrary sense. The formula:

FORMULA: MUTUAL FUNDS CASH/ASSETS RATIO

$$\frac{C}{A} = R$$

> *where C = cash held by mutual funds*
> *A = total assets held by mutual funds*
> *R = cash/assets ratio*

If fund management is exceedingly optimistic and the ratio falls, the contrarian takes that as a sign that market values are going to fall (based on the belief that fund managers are usually wrong). And when the amount of cash rises and the ratio percentage increases, the contrarian begins to think that prices may rise. When this contrarian indicator is combined with a study of new highs and new lows, advance/decline, and observations of volume increasing or decreasing, it works as a technical indicator about the market trend.

Another useful test involving institutional trading is the *large block ratio*. This is a reliable ratio for tracking institutional market activity. A large block (10,000 shares or more) summarizes institutional activity. Financial publications such as the *Wall Street Journal* publish daily summaries of large block trading and total volume. The level of large block trading indicates the level of volume attributed to institutional traders. The formula:

FORMULA: LARGE BLOCK RATIO

$$\frac{B}{V} = R$$

> *where B = large block volume in shares*
> *V = total volume in shares*
> *R = large block ratio*

Like the cash/assets ratio, the large block ratio is popular among contrarian investors. This is based on the belief that mutual funds and other institutional investors are more often wrong about their opinion of market direction. So when the large block ratio begins to increase—meaning more activity among institutions—that implies that the market is more likely to move in the opposite direction.

A deceptive aspect to this assumption is that large block trading may occur when institutions *buy* as well as when they *sell*. The volume itself is a net total of all large block activity. A more revealing trend is a study of advance/decline and new high/new low accompanied by a large block ratio analysis. In this way, you can judge mutual fund volume along with the trend toward issues rising or falling in market value.

The next chapter expands on this discussion by examining and explaining ratios that combine fundamental and technical indicators, and how each side can be used to confirm trends revealed in the other. Ultimately, the best analysis includes a gathering of fundamental *and* technical indicators.

CHAPTER 9

COMBINED TESTING

MERGING PRICE AND FINANCIAL TESTS

THE DEBATE ABOUT WHETHER FUNDAMENTAL OR TECHNICAL ANALYSIS is better or more reliable often polarizes opinions. But you do not have to choose one over the other. The best strategy is to employ both types of tests, for several reasons:

1. *Both approaches offer something of value.* It is not fair to assume that one approach is "correct" and the other is "wrong." Both offer useful information that you need to make good decisions and to time your buy, hold, or sell actions. It is impossible to ignore price trends, even if you are a dedicated, fundamental "true believer." And even the most focused technician understands that financial trends and reports directly affect price. The two cannot be separated, and this indicates that you need to employ both fundamental and technical indicators in managing your portfolio.

2. *Each side is valuable for confirming trends seen in the other.* One valuable use of indicators often ignored in the debate between fundamental and technical proponents is the importance of confirmation. Each side can be used to confirm trends seen emerging in the other. For example, when you see a lot of varia-

tion between reported earnings and core earnings, it implies that you cannot rely on the numbers as much as you'd like. When you see price volatility occurring, it confirms your suspicion. As a trading range broadens and stock price trends begin to look more volatile, you are likely to see a confirming change in reported revenue and earnings.

3. *The two approaches are really different aspects of the same grouping of trends.* Fundamental and technical really come down to degrees of value in a company and its stock. A long-term investor is more likely to ignore short-term price trends and focus primarily on financial information, and a speculator is just as likely to focus only on chart patterns and price-based trends. Realistically, however, these are simply different time frames for the same pricing and valuation issues. Short-term trends are known to be unreliable for long-term forecasting, and speculators accept this as a risk. But those same trends, as chaotic as they are, represent segments of the longer-term trend, and you can begin to understand how those trends evolve by tracking both fundamental and technical indicators.

4. *Some of the most valuable indicators combine fundamental and technical information.* Finally, you cannot avoid using both fundamental and technical indicators. Two of the most popular and valuable indicators already combine both sides. Earnings per share (EPS) compares the fundamental earnings to the technical price per share; and the price/earnings ratio (P/E) represents price as a multiple of earnings. In fact, there are several additional indicators combining price per share with fundamental indicators, and these are explained later in this chapter.

Effective Use of Combined Analysis

The process of *confirmation* is a crucial process for every investor, no matter whether you lean toward speculative or conservative thinking. To effectively time your decisions, you can make good use of combined analysis. You can confirm any apparent trend by checking relevant information on the other side (fundamental versus technical and vice versa).

The technical side will invariably involve comparisons of price; so you may find valuable information comparing prices to the following fundamental indicators:

1. *Changes in revenue and earnings.* The levels of revenue and earnings are reported quarterly. The great "game" on Wall Street is prediction. Analysts consult with corporate management and examine the financial trends and then publish their estimates of earnings, usually expressed in EPS. Remembering that the analyst's opinion is only an estimate, it is disturbing that so much weight is given to it. For example, if a corporation's quarterly earnings exceed its own internal expectations, you would expect the stock value to rise. But if actual reported results are a penny or two per share less than an analyst predicted, that causes the stock to fall.

   Ignoring the game of prediction and reaction, how can you use revenue and earnings information to confirm (or contradict) what you see in the stock's price? As revenue grows, you have every reason to expect net earnings to improve as well. But this does not always occur. So if earnings remain flat or even decline in a period of higher revenue, it is a negative signal. It may explain why a stock's price performance has been weak as well.

   Changes in trading range may also foreshadow disappointments in earnings or, in many cases, positive earnings surprises. For example, if reported earnings are higher than the analysts predicted (or, more importantly, higher than the corporation estimated), that is very positive. And you might see a positive trend in the stock's price, confirming the good news.

2. *Earnings surprises.* The difference of a few pennies between expected earnings and actual earnings is part of the expectation on the market. And when these small adjustments occur, a stock's price may fall or rise for one or two days, usually returning to "normal" levels quickly. But an earnings surprise is somewhat different. For example, if a corporation booked a

large downward adjustment in the latest quarter, earnings may be reported substantially lower than expected. Even with an announcement that future revenue and earnings are expected to be lower than previously announced, a drop in the stock's price confirms the earnings surprise, often months in advance.

This works in the opposite direction as well. A surprise may be a reported higher than predicted level of revenue and earnings, usually based on exceptionally strong sales in the last portion of the quarter. The inevitable result will be higher stock prices, sometimes temporarily and at other times as part of a breakout leading to a higher trading range. The identification of cause and effect is difficult because with every price movement, some stockholders take profits (at the top) or cut losses (at the bottom). So short-term speculation in trading obscures what is going on with long-term investors who follow the fundamentals. On a day-to-day basis, price movement is likely to be chaotic and involve a series of offsetting overreactions to virtually everything. So confirming earnings surprises with observation of trading-range adjustments is a valuable step.

3. *Rumors or news reports concerning mergers and acquisitions.* Wall Street loves rumors and thrives on them. The culture of the market prefers rumor over fact, and investors often make snap decisions on the basis of rumor, without even knowing whether the information is true or false. At the same time, those enthusiasts who encourage rumor also worry constantly about whether their information is reliable. The expression, "Stocks climb a wall of worry" is based not only on the realities of supply and demand, but also on the popularity of the rumor.

One of the favorite rumors is that a particular company is going to be taken over by a competitor. This "merger mania" comes and goes at various times, but the course of the rumor is always the same. The fact that the rumor exists makes it more likely than not that it is true, and traders react accordingly. This gives rise to one of the favorite (but illegal) tactics used by some traders, the "pump and dump." An individual buys a large number of shares in a company and then spreads a rumor (on investment chat lines, for example) that the company is about to be acquired by a larger competitor. This rumor drives up the stock's price (pump), and then the instigator sells (dumps) the stock.

4. *News announcements concerning lawsuits, tax matters, and more.* A bit more tangible than a rumor concerning a merger or acquisition is the reality of contingent liabilities. In recent years, two very large companies have been named as defendants in literally thousands of lawsuits. Altria (MO), the world's largest tobacco company, has been and remains a defendant in lawsuits filed by smokers, states, and the federal government. These suits will not be settled for many years and could end up costing the company billions of dollars. But because the outcome is not known, the problem is only a *contingent* liability. The second company is Merck (MRK), whose Vioxx problems also led to thousands of lawsuits when it was revealed that the prescription drug was far from safe. As in the case of Altria, Merck's actual future liability cannot be known until the thousands of lawsuits run their course.

Merck suffered another contingent problem in 2006 when it was revealed the company might face as much as a $5.58 billion additional tax liability with the United States and Canada. As a result of this story (accompanied by the November 2006 election results), the company's stock fell several points. The liability itself—like the lawsuit liabilities—is contingent, and the final outcome may be far lower, but the contingency itself is enough to cause the stock's price to fall several points.

Valid Versus Invalid Forms of Testing

One of the important assumptions about any form of analysis is that it will yield information that is valuable as well as revealing. For example, there are valid justifications for comparing revenue and expenses or dividends and price, but there is no logical reason to compare accounts receivable to depreciation, or to track a developing trend in fixed overhead compared to intangible assets.

This issue is an important one because, in order for your own program to make sense, you need to be able to achieve the following:

1. *You have to limit the number of indicators you follow.* It would be impossible to track every possible form of analysis. With thousands of possible methods you could use, the sheer weight of information would make it impossible to draw useful conclusions. The greater the number of indicators, the higher the chance you will find contradictory outcomes. You are much better off identifying a very limited number of indicators and tracking them together.

2. *The information has to be readily available.* Another problem with some theories is that the raw information itself is not readily available. For example, even a simple balance sheet item, such as inventory level, is not likely to be published by companies every month, so you will need to use quarterly levels. Physical counts of inventory are not performed routinely either, so the information may not be accessible. This means that a detailed month-to-month average of inventory cannot be part of your program of analysis.

3. *The data you employ have to be current.* Some data are simply outdated by the time you get the information. If you are referring to published financial statements from six months in the past, matters are likely to have changed due to emerging earnings, cyclical realities, and changed markets. Finding current data may rely on estimates and unaudited results, but there is a trade-off between timing and accuracy. This doesn't mean certain ratios should not be calculated; it does mean that current information is not always available, and whatever is published might be modified later.

4. *Data in related sets of information should be comparable, in terms of valuation and time.* A ratio should involve two or more sets of information that are directly related. This applies in two specific ways. The first is valuation; the second is timing. For example, the inventory turnover ratio should be performed comparing inventory to the cost of goods sold because both of these are reported on a cost basis. (Inventory statistics used should be an average for the period in which cost of goods sold

is derived.) However, some analysts prefer comparing inventory values to revenue. The reported revenue total is marked up so inventory is at cost and revenue is at retail. This makes the comparison less reliable because the valuation base is not the same. Proponents of using revenue argue that the mix of cost markup is one feature in tracking turnover, and while this is true, the outcome can be distorted when one line of business is marked up more than another.

Timing is also a crucial factor influencing comparability of data. For example, if you use the traditional P/E ratio, you will be comparing price (current value) to latest-reported earnings, which may be several months old. Invariably, this gap in time makes P/E less reliable than analysts would like. With that in mind, P/E makes sense when compared as a matter of period-specific ending price and earnings (so that P/E can be tracked from quarter to quarter over time). Or current price should be representative of average prices for the last period of time extending back through the earnings period (quarter or year). As an alternative, average mid-trading range price may be compared to estimated current-period earnings. This is an unreliable method because it includes data that are not specific. However, the current-period P/E is always going to be unreliable because it uses information from two different time periods.

5. *You need to be able to act on the information revealed.* Finally, the ratios and formulas you use must be valuable in some way. The outcome of indicated trends must provide you with a conforming or contradicting set of circumstances. For example, if a company's revenues have been rising and earnings keeping pace, this is a positive trend. But if the latest quarter's results show continuing increased revenue but *declining* earnings, this is an indication that something has changed. It warrants further investigation and may signal that a previously positive trend has turned negative.

Identifying Important Combined Tests

The major indicator using a combination of fundamental and technical information is the P/E ratio. The price is shown as a multiple of earnings. So when the P/E is 10, that means that the *current* price is 10 times greater than the *latest* earnings per share.

The problem in relying heavily on this popular ratio is its potentially inaccurate outcome. The problem of distortion is especially severe if and when the interim cycles of an industry have changed since the latest earnings report. For example, in the retail sector, the quarter ending December 31 is usually the highest volume for revenue and earnings, and the March 31 quarter is often the lowest. So if your P/E calculation takes place in March or early April, it could be unreliable. If the current price is compared to the latest reported earnings as of December 31, the entire calculation has been distorted. If the price itself has remained within a narrow trading range but actual current revenue and earnings levels have fallen off, the P/E cannot be assumed to be accurate at all.

Even with the obvious distortion between price and earnings, current P/E remains a popular litmus test of stock values. The historical quarterly and annual P/E are much more revealing, in which a year-end price is compared to that year's earnings. However, even this test makes P/E outdated throughout most of the year.

A solution involves tracking the price of a stock throughout the year. You can calculate and estimate a trend in both stock price and earnings and avoid the inaccuracy of time distortions. However, this only works in those companies with relatively stable price movement and predictable earnings.

For example, a test of Wal-Mart's annual revenue shows that top-line growth has been remarkably consistent:[1]

Year	(in $millions)
2006	312,427
2005	285,222
2004	256,329
2003	244,524
2002	217,799

Earnings were also fairly reliable during this same period, averaging between 3.1% and 3.3%. But when this record is compared to that of other retail corporations, the consistency is not always

---

[1] Wal-Mart annual reports.

found. In the case of Wal-Mart, tracking year-to-year P/E is an easy matter, and because revenue and earnings are so consistent, it is easy to rely on estimates during the year. The same suggestion does not apply to every company in the sector, however.

When you are trying to track P/E but recognize that price or earnings volatility makes the outcome less than reliable, you have some alternatives. These include:

1. *Use P/E along with related and confirming indicators.* All indicators and trends should be confirmed or tested through alternatives. Never rely on any single indicator to make a decision about a stock, recognizing that it is the combination of many different indicators that really points out the relative strength of a company and its stock. So when the apparent P/E seems consistent with the historical trend, confirm this with a check of current quarter revenue, estimated earnings, and other tests. The same applies when the P/E seems off from the average: Why is price more volatile than usual? Are cyclical forces at work? What else has changed?

2. *Compare price volatility to reported earnings versus core earnings.* If the trading range of a stock has broadened since the previous year's range, what does that mean? One way to confirm greater volatility is to track the spread between reported earnings and core earnings. You are likely to see a correlation between price volatility and inconsistency in earnings. As core earnings increase, price volatility is likely to increase as well; and when there is very little adjustment between reported and core earnings, it is more likely that the stock's trading range will be narrow and consistent. While these are generalizations, the indicators may serve as confirming data for the current P/E.

3. *Evaluate historical year-end P/E and price range next to current quarter data.* Does the current P/E seem in line with the historical trend? This is always an important test. If you discover that the current P/E is far out of line with the year-end historical level for P/E, it could be that your information is flawed (comparing old earnings with current price levels). If the price has

spiked above or below historical trading ranges, this could explain how the change has occurred, also indicating that the P/E developed currently is not reliable. If earnings estimates are also unusual compared to historical levels for the same quarter (or based on typical year-end), then the P/E should not be assumed to be a conclusive sign of change in the trend.

4. *Confirm P/E changes by comparing price to revenue, book value per share, and cash.* The next section provides additional ratios for comparison of price data. By using these as well as the traditional P/E analysis, you improve the reliability of your information. For example, if all the indicators wander from established levels, you can conclude that the current price is not typical; current earnings are not typical (or perhaps cyclical and distorting the year-long outcome); or both sides of the ratio are less than reliable. In that case, the information gained from fundamental/technical analysis is not reliable. But when these additional price-based tests provide confirming information about the historical consistency in price-based trends, that strengthens the reliability of the current P/E.

▨ Additional Price-Based Combined Tests

The importance of the P/E ratio in evaluating stocks includes the following points:

1. *It is an efficient method for deciding whether a stock is priced at bargain levels.* The higher the P/E, the more chance a stock is overpriced. Over many years, studies have concluded that lower-P/E stocks outperform higher-P/E stocks. When enthusiasm for a stock drives the price up, the P/E follows, so the multiple of earnings rises as well. An efficient method for narrowing down a field of potential investments is to eliminate stocks above a specific P/E level. For example, you might seek stocks with low price volatility (measured by trading range), dividend yield, revenue and earnings, *and* moderate to low P/E. In this simplified variation of analysis, your rule might be to not even consider stocks whose current P/E is greater than

25, for example. (This assumes that you are also able to eliminate the timing disparities inherent in the P/E.) A more conservative investor may set the bar lower; for example, this investor might not care to look at stocks with P/E above 15.

2. *The ratio is easily understood.* Most people can easily comprehend the significance of earnings multiples. The P/E is popular largely because it is simple, easily computed and tracked, and reliable as a comparable indicator. Many other ratios have to be evaluated based on the industry. For example, profitability in the construction sector is expected to be much lower than in information technology or finance. But the P/E tends to be more universal, so it is an excellent test of pricing across the board.

3. *The P/E can help you to set standards for stocks.* The P/E can also be used to set decision points for buy, hold, or sell decisions. A *range* for P/E is useful for investors, because in ideal circumstances you want some strong market interest (thus, you don't want the P/E to fall too low) while wanting to avoid an unjustified price run-up (so the P/E should not rise too high). Another version of this is a comparison of P/E and core P/E (based on core earnings rather than on reported earnings). The greater the gap between these two, the less reliable the historical P/E. As an alternative test of fundamental volatility (and price volatility), core P/E serves as a way for confirming other emerging trends in price as well as in earnings.

Some additional tests between technical (price) and fundamental results can help to both confirm P/E and expand its significance. The first of these is the *price to revenue ratio*. This test, sometimes called the *revenue multiplier*, is less popular than the P/E ratio but can provide depth in the all-important comparison between price and fundamentals. The current price per share is divided by revenue per share:

FORMULA: PRICE TO REVENUE RATIO

$$\frac{P}{S} = R$$

where P = price per share
  S = sales (revenue) per share
  R = price to revenue ratio

In situations where earnings are flat as a percentage of revenue, but represent a growing dollar value each year, the P/E ratio can become less revealing. As a measurement, P/E has always been assumed as a positive when it remains within a narrow band. However, as long as the number of outstanding shares remains stationary, you would expect the price to revenue ratio to change as revenue levels expand.

A second of the alternative price-based tests is the *price to book value per share*. This compares price at the end of a quarter or year to the reported book value:

FORMULA: PRICE TO BOOK VALUE PER SHARE

$$\frac{P}{B} = R$$

where P = price per share
  B = book value per share
  R = price to book value per share

A problem with book value is what it includes and excludes. Under GAAP, companies are not required to report pension liabilities even when they are huge. At the same time, numerous inflated intangible assets, such as goodwill, distort book value, and the market value of real estate may be far greater than the acquisition price minus depreciation. The price to book by itself is not meaningful, but if you track it as a trend over time, you may discover that a company is being perceived as more valuable or less valuable (based on this ratio). Most analysts agree that market value is a factor of revenue and earnings more than book value, but this serves as a good confirming test.

A more reliable version of this is the *price to tangible book value per share*, in which intangible assets are removed from the equation. This formula at least is more likely to approximate a "liquidation value" of a company, since goodwill and other intangibles cannot be given a sales value. The tangible book value per share is more widely used by analysts than the unadjusted book value, but under GAAP it continues to present problems with accuracy. The formula:

FORMULA: PRICE TO TANGIBLE BOOK VALUE PER SHARE

$$\frac{P}{B - I} = R$$

where P = price per share
B = book value per share
I = intangible assets per share
R = price to tangible book value per share

One final price-based ratio is the *price to cash ratio*. This is a comparison between current price per share and current cash per share. Included in cash are other liquid assets, such as marketable securities—cash plus assets immediately convertible to cash. The formula:

FORMULA: PRICE TO CASH RATIO

$$\frac{P}{C + L} = R$$

where P = price per share
C = cash on hand
L = liquid assets
R = price to cash ratio

Use of cash within a company is going to vary greatly by sector; so this ratio is useful only for tracking a trend within one company, or for comparing companies within a single sector. It is also a valuable confirming test when companies allow their long-term debt to rise while creating an offsetting increase in cash balances. (This keeps the current ratio at desired levels while creating long-term problems for the company.) The price to cash ratio is also a test of how efficiently a company manages its working capital while avoiding inefficient use of cash balances. Thus, the ratio may be tied to a calculation of return on equity and return on invested capital.

The Oddities of Hybrid Analysis

The traditional ratios, such as P/E, are hybrids; this term is used because fundamental and technical analysis are so dissimilar that many people don't consider the viability of combining both. Beyond the P/E, little discussion takes place about combining fundamental and technical analysis. This is true because the two sides are based on different influences and forces:

1. *Price is the result of auction bidding; earnings are not.* The dynamic changes in the price of stock can be described in simple terms. For example, a supply and demand argument tells you that increased supply drives prices down and increased demand drives prices up. But within the realm of supply and demand, an unknown number of forces are at work: knowledge about earnings strength or weakness, changes in management, insider buy or sell decisions, labor disputes, institutional acquisition or disposal or large blocks, good or bad news among a company's competitors, unrest in some part of the world, election results . . . the list can go on endlessly. Price and the influences around it are highly chaotic and unpredictable.

The fundamentals are far more predictable and give a range of possible outcomes. Compared to prices, the fundamentals usually offer very few surprises. You probably know the likely range of EPS for a company you are tracking; revenue and earnings growth is probably going to occur within a known range as well. In companies with volatility in levels of revenue and earnings, investors become uncertain because predictions are difficult if not impossible to make. But compared to price uncertainty, the fundamental tests—especially over many years—reveal trends more dependable than price trends.

2. *The causes of movement in revenue and earnings are finite.* It is reassuring to a fundamental analyst that specific trends need to be tracked and interpreted. The potential cause and effect is a smaller universe than the technical (price-based) cause and effect. Fundamental change in corporate valuation involves capitalization and working capital. Fundamental change in profitability involves study of revenue trends, costs, and expenses. Within that, an analyst considers capitalization, competition, sector strength or weakness, management, and other fundamental realities. The difference between reported and core earnings also affects the analyst's judgment about a company. This does not mean that volatility is always bad news; it does mean that prediction is more difficult when volatility is greater.

3. *Price potentially changes rapidly in either direction based on perceived value; earnings and valuation tend to be more stable and rational.* The changes in price levels can be studied and quantified in many ways. Traditional but overly simplified analyses of price volatility ignore price spikes. A more insightful analysis of typical breadth in trading range is more dependable for identifying price volatility. Combining this with a study of the direction the trading range is moving (prices trending up, down, or flat) is also more revealing than traditional volatility studies. When trading range broadens or narrows, that may also signal changes in the near future. Technical analysis is complex because it requires interpretation without any specific, limited standards.

Fundamental analysis is more likely to be based on a universally understood standard. A current ratio of 2 or better is good; when it slips down below 1 or into negative territory, that is bad. In a particular sector, companies usually report net earnings of 4% to 6%. If a company's profits fall below that, it is negative. Virtually any company wants to report a profit, which is always better than reporting a net loss (in spite of what some annual reports claim to the contrary). Most ratios are the latest entry in a trend. Thus, you can quickly and easily determine whether a trend is positive or negative, or whether the results are reasonably predictable or highly volatile.

With these comparisons and differences in mind, it makes sense to combine both sides of the analytical model. The fundamentals can be more easily interpreted and trends established and followed, but financial reports are historical and out of date by the time you have final data. To find out what is taking place today in a highly erratic and dynamic market, you also need to track the technical trends. Specifically, trading range and its emerging trend, price volatility itself, volume, and the hybrid ratios comparing price to fundamentals are all valuable in confirming fundamental trends, establishing and spotting new trends in price and risk, or setting up an apparent trend for additional confirmation through other tests.

To the extent that you identify useful and insightful forms of hybrid analysis, your overall program is going to improve in the process. For the most part, all analysis is going to improve your estimates; but remember, decisions you make based on analysis are at best informed guesses. Good analysis improves your profits, but there are no guarantees, except one: If you make a profit, the government is going to want its share of that profit. This is the topic of the next chapter.

TAXATION OF INVESTMENTS

UNCLE SAM'S SHARE

ALCULATING NET PROFIT ON INVESTMENTS or tracking corporate profits as reported are by no means simple matters. The variables are many in both instances. On the corporate side, one major factor affecting net earnings is the tax liability the corporation incurs. It is very difficult to make like-kind comparisons between corporations due to the complexities. No two corporations will necessarily have the same tax burden because of:

1. *Tax liabilities or benefits from international operations.* Some corporations operate major segments overseas; others do not. This affects overall tax rates. For example, Altria involves both tobacco and food operations. Altria reports a large source of revenue from international operations. Over five years, Altria and one of its competitors, Reynolds American, reported vastly different effective tax rates:[1]

Year	Reynolds American	Altria
2005	30.4%	29.9%
2004	24.4	32.4

[1] Reynolds American and Altria annual reports.

2003	—	34.9
2002	38.8	35.5
2001	50.2	37.9

2. *Reduced net liabilities caused from carryover losses.* When corporations report large net losses, they may carry those losses forward and apply them against future profits. This complicates the after-tax comparison between companies. That does not mean the tax carryover should not be considered, but it is yet one additional complication in the attempt to make valid comparisons between companies and the yield investors may expect in the future.

3. *Variation in state tax liabilities.* Tax liabilities for corporations vary depending on the state where they are based, and on the many states where they have active operations. If a company has large volume in a state with a higher than average tax rate, then its tax expense will also be larger than average.

There is no single, effective tax rate that can be applied at the corporate level. This is one of many considerations to keep in mind in a program of fundamental analysis. Investors are also keenly aware of their own tax burden and need to calculate the tax consequences within their personal portfolio.

After-Tax Return

As an investor, you probably place most emphasis on a straight return. You invest $1,000 and sell for $1,100, netting 10%. But in fact there are three elements to this return that affect your *real* profit:

1. *Time.* The 10% return you earn in three months actually annualizes out as a 40% return: 10% ÷ 3 months × 12 months = 40%. But annualizing works in the other direction as well. If it takes you two years to earn your 10%, the annualized return is cut in half: 10% ÷ 24 months × 12 months = 5%. Time cannot be ignored as a significant factor in comparing returns between investments.

2. *Inflation.* That time element is further affected by the deterioration in purchasing power. Most people think of inflation as a rise in prices, but this is a coin with two sides. Prices rise because the dollar loses its purchasing power. So if it takes you two years to realize a 10% return and inflation is 3% per year, you also lose purchasing power. A $1,000 investment over two years loses

Year 1 $1,000 × 97% = $970
Year 2 $970 × 97% = $941

The after-inflation value of the original investment loses $59 over two years. So the gross gain of 10% has to be reduced because of inflation:

$100 profit − $59 = $41

If this profit were to take a longer period of time to realize, inflation's bite would be even greater.

3. *Taxes.* Finally, the rate you pay in taxes also reduces the profit. Even a 10% profit can quickly disappear. For example, federal tax rates can be as high as 35%, and state tax rates vary. For example, if you have to pay 35% federal and 6% to your state, that is a significant drop in your profit. When you combine tax liability with inflation, the combined effect can cause that 10% return to evaporate. Based on the assumptions presented above:

Profit before taxes and inflation, 10% of a $1,000 investment	$100
Less: Taxes, federal, 35%	− 35
Taxes, state, 6%	− 6
Inflation (assuming 3% per year, over 2 years)	− 59
Total reductions	$100
After-tax, after-inflation profit	$ 0

The assumed federal and state tax liability is based on the effective tax rate, or the actual rate assessed on taxable income, which is discussed later in this chapter. The point in the example above is to demonstrate that the combined effect of inflation and taxes can be destructive to a return on investment. A 10% return is not only annualized to potentially a much lower rate (the example assumed two years, or 5% per year), but in the year of sale, you suffer not only the federal and state tax effect, but the loss of purchasing power, the invisible loss caused by inflation.

In calculating any return on investment, it makes sense to be aware of these problems. Every investor needs to set personal goals based on what level of return is expected. If you want to achieve a 10% return—an aggressive goal in most cases—then how do you deal with inflation and taxes? Some suggestions:

1. *Invest in a tax-deferred account.* The investments you make through a self-directed IRA or other qualified retirement account are exempt from the year-to-year tax impact. These profits are not taxed until funds are withdrawn in future years. The investments you make in this protected account can achieve your goals without having to be higher to pay taxes to the federal or state government.

2. *Look for ways to shelter some income.* You can either reduce your taxable income or offset investment profits by looking for ways to shelter some of your income. Owning your own home provides itemized deductions for interest and property tax, and can significantly lower your taxable income. Buying investment real estate and renting it out produces cash flow and also provides attractive tax benefits. Real estate is the only investment in which you are allowed to deduct passive losses, up to $25,000 per year. So it is possible to achieve positive cash flow and, at the same time, a tax loss (due to depreciation), which helps you to reduce your tax burden—and if you select real estate in a healthy market, the property value rises while your tenants cover your mortgage payment.

3. *Set after-tax goals lower and more realistically.* You should not expect to realize a post-inflation, post-tax return of 10% unless

you are also willing to take on much higher risks. If your combined federal and state effective tax rate is 41% and you assume 3% inflation per year, you would need to earn about 22.5% to reach your annual goal:

Profit before taxes and inflation, 22.5% of a $1,000 investment	$225
Less: Taxes, federal, 35%	− 79
Taxes, state, 6%	− 14
Inflation (assuming 3%)	− 30
Total reductions	$123
After-tax, after-inflation profit	$102 (10.2%)

An expectation of earning a 22.5% return each and every year is not realistic, so the plan will not work. Most investors will be happy to preserve their spending power while covering taxes, so a return anywhere above 5% accomplishes this goal.

Federal and State Liabilities

The calculation of income tax liability is so varied by state and income level that it is impossible to provide even an estimate of a typical tax rate. In addition, the actual rate depends on personal income level, exemptions, deductions, retirement plans, and carryover losses. Many large U.S. cities also assess a *local* income tax. Among these cities are New York, Baltimore, Columbus, Detroit, and Cincinnati. Maryland counties outside of Baltimore also assess a county income tax.

The decision to trade off income taxes for property taxes is debated in many states, and those states with relatively low tax rates may have higher than average property taxes. This is a complicated subject, but for the purposes of determining an after-tax return on your investments, if you live in a city where income taxes have to be paid, you need to include that liability in your calculation of after-tax profits.

Table 10.1 summarizes the range of federal tax rates, with rates all based on taxable income.

TABLE 10.1. 2005 FEDERAL PERSONAL INCOME TAX RATES.

Tax Rate	Single Filers	Married Filing Jointly or Qualifying Widow/Widower	Married Filing Separately	Head of Household
10%	Up to $7,300	Up to $14,600	Up to $7,300	Up to $10,450
15%	$7,301–$29,700	$14,601–$59,400	$7,301–$29,700	$10,451–$39,800
25%	$29,701–$71,950	$59,401–$119,950	$29,701–$59,975	$39,801–$102,800
28%	$71,951–$150,150	$119,951–$182,800	$59,976–$91,400	$102,801–166,450
33%	$150,151–$326,450	$182,801–$326,450	$91,401–$163,225	$166,451–$326,450
35%	$326,451 or more	$326,451 or more	$163,226 or more	$326,451 or more

The state tax rate has to be included in the calculation of after-tax income from your investments. State ranges of income tax rates are summarized in Table 10.2. Many states include different brackets for single or married people, and other rules and exceptions (such as tax-free earnings up to a specified amount) might also apply.

VALUABLE RESOURCES:

To check the rules in detail in your state, check the Web sites for the Federation of Tax Administrators, www.taxadmin.org/fta/rate/ind_inc.html and State Tax Central at www.statetaxcentral.com.

The actual range of tax liability you will experience in your state depends on your income and filing status, and there is no specific "high state" or "low state" except those few states that have no income tax or that tax only interest and dividends. The range of rates is quite varied. The highest low-end rate is North Carolina, where the tax burden starts out at 6% (however, the first $12,749 of income is exempt). The highest high-end rate is in Vermont, where the tax rate can be as high as 9.5%.

In both federal and state calculations, the definition of taxable income and effective tax rate are the same. Taxable income is the remainder when gross income is reduced by adjustments to gross income, itemized or standard deductions, and exemptions. The effective tax rate is the rate paid on taxable income. In some states, rules for the calculation of taxable income are not identical to fed-

TABLE 10.2. 2005 STATE INCOME TAX RATES.

State	Tax rates		State	Tax rates	
	Low	High		Low	High
Alabama	2.00%	5.00%	Alaska	no state income tax	
Arizona	2.87	5.04	Arkansas	1.0%	7.00%
California	1.00	9.30	Colorado	4.63 flat rate	
Connecticut	3.00	5.00	Delaware	2.20	5.95
Florida	no state income tax		Georgia	1.00	6.00
Hawaii	1.40	8.25	Idaho	1.60	7.80
Illinois	3.00 flat rate		Indiana	3.40 flat rate	
Iowa	0.36	8.98	Kansas	3.50	6.45
Kentucky	2.00	6.00	Louisiana	2.00	6.00
Maine	2.00	8.50	Maryland	2.00	4.75
Massachusetts	5.30 flat rate		Michigan	3.90 flat rate	
Minnesota	5.35	7.85	Mississippi	3.00	5.00
Missouri	1.50	6.00	Montana	1.00	6.90
Nebraska	2.56	6.84	Nevada	no state income tax	
New Hampshire	tax only on dividends and interest		New Jersey	1.40	8.97
New Mexico	1.70	5.30	New York	4.00	6.85
North Carolina	6.00	8.25	North Dakota	2.10	5.54
Ohio	0.712	7.185	Oklahoma	0.50	6.25
Oregon	5.00	9.00	Pennsylvania	3.07 flat rate	
Rhode Island	25% of federal tax		South Carolina	2.50	7.00
South Dakota	no state income tax		Tennessee	tax only on dividends and interest	
Texas	no state income tax		Utah	2.30	7.00
Vermont	3.60	9.50	Virginia	2.00	5.75
Washington	no state income tax		West Virginia	3.00	6.50
Wisconsin	4.60	6.75	Wyoming	no state income tax	
DC	4.50	9.00			

eral rules. For example, the lower federal rate for long-term capital gains (see explanation below) may not apply equally in state tax rules. This means that in order to calculate the true tax liability based on large capital gains in a single year, you need to perform two separate calculations. The states also apply their own rules for taxation of dividends. The Tax Act of 2003 changed the federal rules. From that time onward, dividends are taxed at the same rate as long-term capital gains, 5% for some and 15% for most people.

Even when the effective tax rate is calculated, it applies only to ordinary income (from salary and wages, self-employment, etc.) but not on capital gains or dividends, where rates are lower.

The Tax Act of 2003 changed the rules for long-term capital gains. A long-term gain is defined as a gain on any asset owned more than one year. For example, if you held stock for 13 months and then sold it at a profit, your tax rate on the profit would most likely be 15% (some lower-income people would pay only 5%).

Deferred Tax Planning

The tax rules are complex, and when you consider both federal and state together, the total cost of taxes is considerable. A family with taxable income above $190,000 will be taxed at 33%, and this level of income in a two-income family is not unusual. When you add in a typical 5% state tax, the total penalty is 38% of taxable income. On $150,000, that is $72,200 in annual taxes.

With this in mind, careful advance tax planning is essential, and a little time invested is likely to reduce your tax burden. Some suggestions:

1. *Time capital gains with taxes in mind.* You have control over the timing of capital gains. In years where your taxable income will be high, avoid selling stocks and accumulating a larger tax debt. Also try to hold stocks long enough so that larger gains are long-term, so that you achieve the favored rates.

2. *Match capital gains with losses in the same year.* If you are planning to sell stock this year and report a gain, try to match it with a capital loss at the same time. If you have stocks in your portfolio whose performance has lagged, matching gains and losses is a sensible way to avoid taxes.

3. *Seek high-dividend stocks as an alternative to interest income.* If you invest a portion of your capital in certificates of deposit (CDs), you may reduce taxes by replacing these with high-yielding stocks. While dividends are taxed at favorable lower rates, interest is not. So you can reduce your tax burden by locating stocks with dividends at the same yield as those CDs.

4. *Maximize tax-deferred investment whenever possible.* Invest the maximum allowed in your IRA and other tax-deferred accounts. Long-term capital gains are not especially useful in a tax-deferred account, but income taxed at your full rate (such as short-term capital gains and interest) is appropriate in a self-directed retirement account.

5. *Diversify into real estate investments to reduce taxes.* The tax benefits of real estate should not be ignored in your diversified portfolio. Investment real estate losses can be deducted to as high as $25,000 per year. In addition, you can sell a primary residence as often as once every two years and all the profits (up to $500,000 for a married couple or $250,000 for a single person) are exempt from federal tax.

The range of tax benefits and consequences is a complication for anyone who invests money in the stock market. For most, the services of a qualified and experienced tax professional are needed just to comply with the law. The same professional should also be qualified to help you with your tax planning so that future taxes are kept to the legal minimum.

All aspects of investing—including taxes—require diligence and research. To the extent that you are able to apply the formulas and ratios investors need and use, your analytical base of information improves. This applies on multiple levels, as this book has demonstrated. The two major areas of interest to you are:

1. *Corporate profitability and valuation.* The task of determining which companies are strongest in terms of long-term profitability, and which ones hold out the strongest valuation for investors, is by no means simple. It should be, but the accounting rules obscure many facts rather than reveal them. A few key ratios and formulas can help you to cut through the veil of technical reporting to find the truth.

2. *Stock analysis.* Whether you like the fundamentals or the technical, or use a combination of both, analysis can become complex and confusing. For this reason, it makes sense to identify a very limited number of valuable tests and use them in con-

junction to test, verify, and confirm the trends you spot. Beating the market is not as easy as some people try to make it sound; but smart use of a few indicators definitely will improve your odds, leading to higher profits and lower risks.

No one can promise you the certainty investors would like without also considering the risk levels involved. The higher the opportunity for profit, the higher the risk. These relationships are unavoidable, but the use of those all-important ratios and formulas can help you select the proper range for your situation, identify the means for picking the best stocks, and know when to sell and take your profits.

Stock Market Formulas: Summarizing the Essentials

ACCOUNTS RECEIVABLE TURNOVER

$$\frac{S}{A} = T$$

where S = credit sales
A = accounts receivable
T = accounts receivable turnover

ACCUMULATED VALUE

$$P\,(1\,+\,R)^n = A$$

where P = principal amount
R = interest rate
n = number of periods
A = accumulated value

ACCUMULATED VALUE PER PERIOD

$$P\left(\frac{((1 + R)^n - 1)}{R}\right) = A$$

where P = principal amount
R = interest rate
n = number of periods
A = accumulated value

ACCUMULATED VALUE WITH COMPOUNDING

$$\frac{R}{P(1 + (R \div D))^n} = A$$

where P = principal amount
R = interest rate
D = division based on compounding method
n = number of periods
A = accumulated value

ADJUSTED DEBT RATIO

$$\frac{D + S}{C} = R$$

where D = long-term debt
S = mandatorily redeemable preferred stock
C = total capitalization
R = adjusted debt ratio

ADJUSTED VOLATILITY

$$\frac{(H - L) - S}{L} = V$$

where H = 52-week high price
L = 52-week low price
S = price spikes
V = adjusted volatility

ADVANCE/DECLINE RATIO

$$\frac{A}{D} = R$$

where A = number of advancing issues
D = number of declining issues
R = advance/decline ratio

AFTER-TAX INCOME

$$I \times \frac{(100 - R)}{100} = A$$

where I = income before taxes
R = effective tax rate
A = after-tax income

AMORTIZATION PAYMENTS

$$B\left(\frac{1}{V^n}\right) = P$$

where B = balance due on a loan
V = present value per period
n = number of periods
P = payment required

ANNUALIZED RATE

$$\frac{R}{M} = A$$

where R = net return
       M = months the position was open
       A = annualized yield

ANNUALIZED TOTAL RETURN IF EXERCISED

$$\left(\frac{C + O + D}{B} \div H\right) \times 12 = R$$

where C = capital gain
       O = option premium
       D = dividend income
       B = original basis in stock
       H = holding period in months
       R = annualized total return

AVERAGE

$$\frac{O^1 + O^2 + \cdots + O^n}{E} = A$$

where O = outcomes
       E = number of entries (^{n})
       A = average

AVERAGE COLLECTION PERIOD

$$\frac{R}{S \div 365} = D$$

where R = accounts receivable
       S = annual credit sales
       D = average collection period (days)

AVERAGE INVENTORY

$$\frac{I^a + I^b + \cdots + I^n}{n} = A$$

where I = inventory value

a, b = period used in calculation

n = total number of periods

A = average inventory

BAD DEBTS TO ACCOUNTS RECEIVABLE RATIO

$$\frac{B}{A} = R$$

where B = bad debts reserve

A = accounts receivable

R = bad debts to accounts receivable ratio

BOOK VALUE PER SHARE

$$\frac{N - P}{S} = B$$

where N = net worth

P = preferred stock

S = average shares issued and outstanding

B = book value per share

BREAKEVEN RETURN

$$\frac{I}{100 - R} = B$$

where I = rate of inflation

R = effective tax rate (federal and state)

B = breakeven return

CASH RATIO

$$\frac{C + M}{L} = R$$

where C = cash
M = marketable securities
L = current liabilities
R = cash ratio

CHANGE IN VOLUME

$$\frac{(C - P)}{P} = V$$

where C = current period volume
P = past period volume
V = change in volume

COMMON STOCK RATIO

$$\frac{S}{C} = R$$

where S = common stock issued and outstanding
C = total capitalization
R = common stock ratio

CORE DEBT RATIO

$$\frac{L}{T + (-) A} = C$$

where L = long-term debt
T = total capitalization
A = core valuation adjustments
C = core debt ratio

CORE EARNINGS PER SHARE

$$\frac{N + (-)\, A}{S} = C$$

where N = net earnings
A = core earnings adjustments
S = shares outstanding
C = core earnings per share

CORE NET WORTH

$$N + (-)\, A + (-)\, L = C$$

where N = net worth as reported
A = adjustments to reported value of assets
L = adjustments to reported value of liabilities
C = core net worth

CORE P/E RATIO

$$\frac{P}{E + (-)\, A} = C$$

where P = price per share
E = earnings per share as reported
A = core earnings adjustments
C = core P/E ratio

CORE RETURN ON EQUITY

$$\frac{C}{E} = R$$

where C = core earnings (profit) for a one-year period
E = shareholders' equity
R = core return on equity

CORE RETURN ON TOTAL CAPITALIZATION

$$\frac{C + I}{E + B} = R$$

where C = core earnings (profit) for a one-year period
I = interest paid on long-term bonds
E = shareholders' equity
B = par value of long-term bonds
R = core return on total capitalization

CORE TANGIBLE BOOK VALUE PER SHARE

$$\frac{N - P - I + (-)\, C}{S} = B$$

where N = net worth
P = preferred stock
I = intangible assets
C = core net worth adjustments
S = average shares issued and outstanding
B = core tangible book value per share

CURRENT RATIO

$$\frac{A}{L} = R$$

where A = current assets
L = current liabilities
R = current ratio

DAILY COMPOUNDING (ACTUAL DAYS)

$$(1 + (R \div 365))^{365} = I$$

where R = stated interest rate
I = annual percentage rate (APR)

DAILY COMPOUNDING (BANKING METHOD)

$$(1 + (R \div 360))^{360} = I$$

where R = stated interest rate
I = annual percentage rate (APR)

DEBT RATIO

$$\frac{D}{C} = R$$

where D = long-term debt
C = total capitalization
R = debt ratio

DECLINING-BALANCE DEPRECIATION

$$\left(\frac{B - P}{R}\right) \times A = D$$

where B = basis of asset
P = prior depreciation deducted
R = recovery period
A = acceleration percentage
D = annual depreciation

DIVIDEND PAYOUT RATIO

$$\frac{D}{E} = R$$

where D = dividend per share
E = earnings per share
R = dividend payout ratio

DIVIDEND YIELD

$$\frac{D}{P} = Y$$

where D = dividend per share
P = current price per share
Y = dividend yield

EARNINGS PER SHARE

$$\frac{N}{S} = E$$

where N = net earnings
S = shares outstanding
E = earnings per share

EFFECTIVE TAX RATE (FEDERAL)

$$\frac{L}{T} = R$$

where L = liability for taxes
T = taxable income
R = effective tax rate

EFFECTIVE TAX RATE (TOTAL)

$$\frac{FL + SL + LL}{T} = R$$

where FL = liability for taxes, federal
SL = liability for taxes, state
LL = liability for taxes, local
T = taxable income (on federal return)
R = effective tax rate, total

GROSS MARGIN

$$\frac{G}{R} = M$$

where G = gross profit
R = revenue
M = gross margin

INTEREST

$$P \times R \times T = I$$

where P = principal
R = interest rate
T = time
I = interest

INTEREST EXPENSE

$$P \times R = I$$

where P = principal amount
R = annual rate
I = interest (per year)

INVENTORY TURNOVER

$$\frac{C}{A} = T$$

where C = cost of goods sold (annual)
A = average inventory
T = turnover

LARGE BLOCK RATIO

$$\frac{B}{V} = R$$

where B = large block volume in shares
V = total volume in shares
R = large block ratio

MARKET CAPITALIZATION

$$S \times P = C$$

> where S = shares issued and outstanding
> P = price per share
> C = market capitalization

MONTHLY COMPOUNDING

$$(1 + (R \div 12))^{12} = I$$

> where R = stated interest rate
> I = annual percentage rate (APR)

MUTUAL FUNDS CASH/ASSETS RATIO

$$\frac{C}{A} = R$$

> where C = cash held by mutual funds
> A = total assets held by mutual funds
> R = cash/assets ratio

NET AFTER-TAX ANNUALIZED RETURN

$$\left(I \times \frac{100 - R}{100} \div M \right) \times 12 = A$$

> where I = income from investments
> R = effective tax rate (federal and state)
> M = months held
> A = net after-tax annualized return

NET RETURN ON EQUITY

$$\frac{P}{E - S} = R$$

> where P = *profit for a one-year period*
> E = *shareholders' equity*
> S = *mandatorily redeemable preferred stock*
> R = *net return on equity*

NEW HIGH/NEW LOW RATIO

$$\frac{H}{L} = R$$

> where H = *number of issues with new high prices*
> L = *number of issues with new low prices*
> R = *new high/new low ratio*

OPERATING PROFIT MARGIN

$$\frac{E}{R} = M$$

> where E = *expenses*
> R = *revenue*
> M = *operating profit margin*

PERCENTAGE PRICE CHANGE

$$\frac{C}{O} = P$$

> where C = *change*
> O = *opening price*
> P = *percentage price change*

PREFERRED STOCK RATIO

$$\frac{P}{C} = R$$

where P = preferred stock
C = total capitalization
R = preferred stock ratio

PRESENT VALUE

$$F\left(\frac{1}{(1 + R)^n}\right) = P$$

where F = fund value
R = interest rate
n = number of periods
P = present value

PRESENT VALUE PER PERIOD

$$W\left[\left(1 - \frac{1}{(1 + R)^n}\right) \div R\right] = P$$

where W = withdrawals in the future
R = interest rate
n = number of periods
P = present value per period

PRICE/EARNINGS RATIO

$$\frac{P}{E} = R$$

where P = price per share
E = earnings per share
R = P/E ratio

PRICE TO BOOK VALUE PER SHARE

$$\frac{P}{B} = R$$

where P = price per share
B = book value per share
R = price to book value per share

PRICE TO CASH RATIO

$$\frac{P}{C + L} = R$$

where P = price per share
C = cash on hand
L = liquid assets
R = price to cash ratio

PRICE TO REVENUE RATIO

$$\frac{P}{S} = R$$

where P = price per share
S = sales (revenue) per share
R = price to revenue ratio

PRICE TO TANGIBLE BOOK VALUE PER SHARE

$$\frac{P}{B - I} = R$$

where P = price per share
B = book value per share
I = intangible assets per share
R = price to tangible book value per share

PRINCIPAL AND INTEREST ON A MONTHLY PAYMENT

Interest

$$B\left(\frac{R}{12}\right) = I$$

Principal

$$T - I = P$$

New balance forward

$$B - P = N$$

> where B = balance forward
> R = annual interest rate
> I = interest amount
> T = total monthly payment
> P = principal
> N = new balance forward

QUARTERLY COMPOUNDING

$$(1 + (R \div 4))^4 = I$$

> where R = stated interest rate
> I = annual percentage rate (APR)

QUICK ASSETS RATIO

$$\frac{A - I}{L} = R$$

> where A = current assets
> I = inventory
> L = current liabilities
> R = quick assets ratio

RATE OF GROWTH IN CORE EARNINGS

$$\frac{CC - PC}{PC} = E$$

where CC = *current year core earnings*
PC = *past year core earnings*
E = *rate of growth in core earnings*

RATE OF GROWTH IN EXPENSES

$$\frac{C - P}{P} = E$$

where C = *current year expenses*
P = *past year expenses*
E = *rate of growth in expenses*

RATE OF GROWTH IN NET EARNINGS

$$\frac{C - P}{P} = E$$

where C = *current year net earnings*
P = *past year net earnings*
E = *rate of growth in net earnings*

RATE OF GROWTH IN OPERATING PROFIT

$$\frac{C - P}{P} = R$$

where C = *current year operating profit*
P = *past year operating profit*
R = *rate of growth in operating profit*

RATE OF GROWTH IN REVENUE

$$\frac{C - P}{P} = R$$

where C = current year revenue
P = past year revenue
R = rate of growth in revenue

RATIO OF EXPENSES TO REVENUE

$$\frac{E}{R} = P$$

where E = expenses
R = revenue
P = ratio (percentage)

RETURN IF EXERCISED

$$\frac{S - I}{I - O} = R$$

where S = sales price of stock
I = invested capital
O = option premium received
R = return

RETURN ON EQUITY

$$\frac{P}{E} = R$$

where P = profit for a one-year period
E = shareholders' equity
R = return on equity

RETURN ON INVESTED CAPITAL

$$\frac{S - I}{I} = R$$

where S = sales price
I = invested capital
R = return

RETURN ON INVESTMENT NET OF MARGIN

$$\frac{V - B - I}{C} = R$$

where V = current market value
B = basis (including leveraged portion)
I = interest cost
C = current market value at time of sale
R = return on investment net of margin

RETURN ON LONG OPTIONS

$$\frac{S - P}{P} = R$$

where S = closing net sales price
P = opening net purchase price
R = net return

RETURN ON NET INVESTMENT

$$\frac{S - I - C}{I} = R$$

where S = sales price
I = invested capital
C = costs
R = return

RETURN ON NET INVESTMENT WITH NET COST BASIS

$$\frac{S - I}{I + C} = R$$

where S = sales price
     I = invested capital
     C = costs
     R = return

RETURN ON PURCHASE PRICE

$$\frac{S - P}{P} = R$$

where S = sales price
     P = purchase price
     R = return

RETURN ON TOTAL CAPITALIZATION

$$\frac{P + I}{E + B} = R$$

where P = profit for a one-year period
     I = interest paid on long-term bonds
     E = shareholders' equity
     B = par value of long-term bonds
     R = return on equity

SEMIANNUAL COMPOUNDING

$$(1 + (R \div 2))^2 = I$$

where R = stated interest rate
     I = annual percentage rate (APR)

SHORT INTEREST RATIO

$$\frac{S}{V} = R$$

where S = number of shares sold short
V = total trading volume
R = short interest ratio

SINKING FUND PAYMENTS

$$F\left(\frac{1}{(((1 + R)^n - 1) \div R)}\right) = S$$

where F = fund value
R = interest rate
n = number of periods
S = sinking fund payments

STRAIGHT-LINE DEPRECIATION

$$\frac{A}{R} = D$$

where A = basis of asset
R = recovery period
D = annual depreciation

TANGIBLE BOOK VALUE PER SHARE

$$\frac{N - P - I}{S} = B$$

where N = net worth
P = preferred stock
I = intangible assets
S = average shares issued and outstanding
B = tangible book value per share

TAXABLE INCOME

(1) $I - A = G$
(2) $G - E - D = T$

where I = total income, all sources
A = adjustments
G = adjusted gross income
E = exemptions
D = deductions (itemized or standard)
T = taxable income

TOTAL RETURN

$$\frac{S - I - C + D}{I} = R$$

where S = sales price
I = invested capital
C = costs
D = dividends earned
R = return

VOLATILITY

$$\frac{H - L}{L} = V$$

where H = 52-week high price
L = 52-week low price
V = volatility

WEIGHTED AVERAGE CAPITAL

$$\frac{(p^1 \times v) + (p^2 \times v)}{p^t} = W$$

where p^1 = period 1 (number of months)
p^2 = period 2 (number of months)
v = value
p^t = total periods (months in the year)
W = weighted average capital

WORKING CAPITAL TURNOVER

$$\frac{R}{A - L} = T$$

where R = one year's revenue
A = current assets
L = current liabilities
T = working capital turnover

Glossary of Terms

accounts payable   A current liability representing the dollar amount of all currently due bills for a company.

accounts receivable   A current asset (minus a reserve for bad debts) reporting the amount currently due from a company's customers.

accumulated depreciation   An asset account reducing the gross basis of capital assets and offsetting the sum of annual depreciation expenses.

accumulated value   The value of a fund after a period of time, assuming a rate of interest and compounding method.

acid test   Alternate name for the quick assets ratio, the division of current asserts without inventory by current liabilities.

after-tax income   Net income from investments after deducting all applicable income tax liabilities.

amortization   The annual expensing of an asset set up in one year, but applying over two years or more (such as a three-year insurance premium paid in one installment).

annual report   A document published each year by companies that includes financial statements and footnotes; explanations of trends and products provided by management; and descriptions of the company's primary business and segments, markets, and officers.

225

assets   Properties owned by companies, including current assets (cash and assets convertible to cash within 12 months), capital assets net of accumulated depreciation, deferred and prepaid assets, and intangible assets.

bad debts   Accounts receivable written off as expenses because they have become uncollectible.

balance sheet   A financial statement prepared as of a specific date, usually the end of a fiscal quarter or year, reporting the ending balances of all asset, liability, and net worth accounts. The sum of liabilities and net worth equals the sum of all assets.

bonds   Forms of liability reported on the balance sheet as long-term obligations; debt capitalization representing contractual obligations to bondholders for periodic interest payments as well as repayment of the bond face value by a specified deadline.

book value per share   A company's total net worth divided by the number of common shares issued and outstanding.

breakeven return   The return needed to break even after considering the effects of both inflation and taxes.

breakout   An important signal in technical analysis, in which the price of a stock moves above resistance or below support.

call   An option granting its owner the right to buy 100 shares of stock at a fixed price.

capital assets   Those assets reported on a company's balance sheet subject to depreciation over many years, including real estate, vehicles, machinery and equipment, furniture, computers, and tools.

capital stock   The equity value of a company held by stockholders, reported as the value of shares outstanding in one or more classes of common and preferred stock.

capitalization The total funding of a company, consisting of equity (capital stock) and long-term debt (bonds and notes).

cash flow The movement of funds into and out of a company; tests of cash flow indicate the company's ability to pay current liabilities and fund growth.

comparative financial statement A statement including information for the current period as well as the previous period (quarter-to-quarter or year-to-year).

confirmation A process of verifying an indicated trend or change in a trend through a separate indicator.

consolidated financial statement A financial statement including information for the entire company, including all subsidiaries.

contingent liability A liability that may or may not become an actual liability in the future, such as the potential losses from lawsuits.

contrarian investing A strategy in which decisions are made specifically opposite the decisions of the majority, in the belief that the majority is usually wrong.

core earnings Those earnings derived from a company's primary (core) business and excluding nonrecurring sources such as the sale of assets or segments, or accounting adjustments; and including expenses not reported under current accounting rules.

core net worth The true dollar value net worth of a company, including all assets and liabilities not reported on the balance sheet, and with adjustments to reflect the true market value of assets.

cost of goods sold The direct costs incurred by a company, including materials purchased and direct labor, the level of which is expected to track revenue closely.

covered call A call sold when the seller also owns 100 shares of stock for each option.

current assets and liabilities Those assets that are in the form of cash or are convertible to cash within 12 months (accounts receivable, securities, and inventory); and those liabilities that are payable within the next 12 months (accounts payable for current expenses, taxes, and 12 months' payments of long-term obligations).

current ratio A ratio testing working capital; current assets are divided by current liabilities to test a company's conditions against a commonly applied standard of "2" or better as acceptable.

current yield The percentage yield investors earn from dividends, based on the dividend per share divided by the current price per share.

debt ratio An important test of capitalization; long-term debt is divided by total capitalization (long-term debt and net worth), and the result is expressed as a percentage.

deferred assets Any assets that will eventually be reclassified as expenses, either in a single year or over a period of years.

depreciation An annual reduction in the book value of capital assets and reflection of the annual claim as an expense; the term, or recovery period.

diversification Dividing investment capital among different investments and markets, to avoid the risk of loss in an entire portfolio due to a single negative turn.

dividend yield The current yield on stock based on declared dividends. The dividend per share is divided by the current price per share, with the result expressed as a percentage.

Dow Theory   A technical market theory based on tracking of primary movements in indices and confirmation of indicated trends, based on the writings of Charles Dow.

earnings per share (EPS)   The dollar amount of earnings when divided by the number of common shares issued and outstanding during the same period. When the number of shares has changed during the year, an average for the year is used.

effective tax rate   The rate an individual pays based on net taxable income, after deducting exemptions and itemized or standard deduction.

efficient market theory   A theory stating that the current prices of all stocks include all known information about the company at all times; the theory that pricing is the direct result of public knowledge.

equity   The ownership value of a company, as opposed to debt; net worth.

expenses   Payments made by a company for sales or general obligations, including rent, salaries and wages, telephone, office supplies, travel, advertising, and legal fees.

financial statements   The periodic reports published by companies, including the balance sheet (summary of ending balances in asset, liability, and net worth accounts), income statement (revenue, costs, expenses, and profits for the period), and statement of cash flows (a summary of the movement of cash into and out of the company during the reported period).

fiscal year   The year used by corporations to report financial results, which does not necessarily correspond to the calendar year.

footnotes   A section of a company's annual report providing detailed explanations, expansions, and disclosures of items shown on the financial statements.

fundamental analysis   Investment analysis based on financial and related information, including financial statements, dividend declarations and payments, management, competition, and product news.

GAAP   Generally accepted accounting principles, a series of opinions, publications, and rulings issued by several organizations (primarily the AICPA and FASB) mandating the rules for interpreting a company's financial transactions and performing audits.

gaps   Spaces between a stock's trading range from one day to the next, viewed as significant by technicians if those gaps establish a movement out of the current trading range.

goodwill   An intangible asset, an estimated value assigned to the reputation of a company and its product or service.

gross margin   The percentage of gross profit divided by revenue.

gross profit   The dollar value remaining when the cost of goods sold is subtracted from revenue.

head and shoulders   A chart formation popular among technicians, indicating a coming move away from the established trading range.

income statement   A financial statement reporting revenue, costs, expenses, and profits for a specified period of time, usually a fiscal quarter or year.

institutional investor   Any investor in the market with the combined capital of many individuals, such as mutual funds, insurance companies, and pension plans; institutional investors represent the majority of trades and dollar value of the stock market.

intangible assets   Any assets reported on a company's balance sheet that lack tangible value, including goodwill, non-compete covenants, trademarks, and organizational expenses.

inventory turnover A calculation of the average number of times inventory is replaced during a year; a ratio testing inventory efficiency.

large blocks Trades of 10,000 or more shares in a single transaction, usually executed by institutional investors.

liquidity The availability of working capital based on comparisons between current assets and current liabilities.

long-term assets Alternative name for capital assets, or fixed assets; properties set up as assets and depreciated over a recovery period.

long-term liabilities All liabilities due beyond the next 12 months, including long-term notes, contracts, and bonds.

margin An expression of return in the form of a percentage, such as gross margin (gross profit as a percentage of sales), operating margin, or pretax margin.

market capitalization The value of a listed company, or the sum of total shares outstanding multiplied by the current price per share.

market value The current value of an asset on the market, in the event of an immediate sale.

moving average An average in which the latest fields are added and older fields are dropped from the calculation.

multiple The number of times earnings are reflected in the stock's current price. Price per share is divided by earnings per share (the P/E ratio) to find the multiple.

net income The income after all costs and expenses are deducted from revenues.

net profit   The bottom line of profit after all adjustments and taxes.

net return   A percentage calculated by dividing net income by revenues.

net worth   The value of a company including capital stock and retained earnings; the remaining value when total liabilities are deducted from total assets.

operating profit   The profit strictly from operations and excluding other income and expenses and tax liabilities.

option   an intangible contract granting its owner the right to buy or sell 100 shares of stock at a fixed price and before a specified expiration date.

other income and expenses   All adjustments to operating profit for nonoperating items, including interest income and expense, currency exchange gains or losses, and profit or loss from selling capital assets.

P/E ratio   Also called the price/earnings ratio, a popular test of a stock's risk and demand on the market; price per share is divided by earnings per share to calculate a multiple, reported as a single number.

premium   The cost or value of an option.

prepaid assets   Any assets paid in advance of the applicable period; these are set up on the balance sheet and amortized over a period of time so that the expense is reported in the proper accounting year.

present value   The value today of a future fund, based on interest rate and compounding method.

put   An option granting its owner the right to sell 100 shares of stock at a fixed price.

qualified opinion An opinion expressed as a final step in an independent audit, including specific reservations about the accuracy or fairness of a company's financial statements.

quick assets ratio Also called the acid test ratio, a comparison between current assets (excluding inventory) and current liabilities; a variation of the current ratio.

random walk hypothesis A theory stating that all stock price movement is random and cannot be predicted accurately, because price change results only from supply and demand.

ratio Generally, any abbreviated form of expression concerning two related financial outcomes, expressed as a percentage or a single number.

reserve for bad debts An account reducing the balance sheet value of accounts receivable to anticipate likely levels of bad debt expenses.

resistance The top of a stock's trading range, or the highest price buyers are willing to pay for shares based on current conditions.

retail investor The individual, a non-institutional investor.

return Profit from investing in stocks or, in the reporting by companies, profit remaining after costs and expenses are deducted from revenue.

revenues The gross income, or sales, reported by a company during a specified period of time (fiscal quarter or year), before deductions of costs or expenses.

shareholders' equity The net worth of a company, equal to the net difference between total assets and total liabilities.

simple average An average calculated without adjustments, in which a number of values are added together and then divided by the total count of values.

sinking fund payments   The amount of periodic payments needed to accumulate a sum at the end, based on frequency of payments, interest rate, and compounding method.

spike   In statistics, an aberration in a trend above or below more typical entries. Spikes are normally removed from any calculations such as averages or price ranges.

statement of cash flows   The third financial statement (included with the balance sheet and income statement), which summarizes all sources and applications of funds and provides details between beginning and ending balances of cash.

statement of operations   Alternative name for the income statement.

stockholders' equity   The total equity value of a company, also representing the net difference between total assets and total liabilities.

support   The lowest price in a stock's trading range; the lowest price at which investors are willing to sell under current conditions.

swing trading   A technical trading strategy based on two- to five-day price trends, identification of buy and sell set-up signals, and chart tracking to time decisions.

tangible book value per share   The net worth of a company minus intangible assets, divided by the number of shares issued and outstanding.

technical analysis   All forms of analysis based on a stock's price and price movement and trend, including patterns in price charts, trading range, and volume.

total capitalization   The sum of long-term liabilities (debt capitalization) and shareholders' equity (equity capitalization).

trading range The price difference between the trend in the highest and lowest prices of a stock under current conditions.

trend Any factor followed by investors, either fundamental or technical, that is tracked and monitored over time.

volatility An expression of a stock's risk, usually based on a comparison of high and low prices over a 12-month period.

weighted average capital The dollar value of capital calculated to account for changes in level at various times during the year.

weighted moving average Any moving average in which some fields (usually the most recent) are given greater weight than others.

working capital Funds available to a corporation to pay its bills and fund growth, consisting of the net difference between current assets and current liabilities.

yield The margin, profit, or return; used by corporations to indicate yield in the form of dividends or based on profits compared to revenues, and used by investors to calculate profit or loss on invested funds.

INDEX